WHAT READERS OF
THE GOOD FIGHT
ARE SAYING

The Good Fight changed everything in our relationship. It's the first book we've actually looked forward to reading together.

THOMAS AND MELISSA, MARRIED 17 YEARS

Who knew conflict could be fun? We laughed out loud while reading this book. And, thanks to the app, we're now practicing "The Rules of Fight Club." *The Good Fight* delivers!

JUSTIN AND BELLA, MARRIED 5 YEARS

The chapter about your personal "Fight Type" is worth the price of the whole book. One of us is a "Cautious Fighter" and the other is a "Competitive Fighter." That awareness was a game-changer in our marriage.

COLIN AND MARIA, MARRIED 33 YEARS

We don't fight a lot but when we do it's usually a doozy. Les and Leslie taught us how to turn those tough times around faster than we ever imagined. We love *The Good Fight*.

MARCO AND CARRIE, MARRIED 14 YEARS

The first time we heard Les and Leslie say that you can use conflict to bring you closer together, we had our doubts. But after reading *The Good Fight*, we are true believers. Our relationship has never been better.

DANIEL AND KATHY, MARRIED 6 YEARS

We've never read a book like this. The app is incredible because it actually has us put into practice what we're reading. Genius!

To be honest, we never thought about the difference between a good fight and a bad fight. That first chapter opened our eyes—especially when it comes to our long-standing fights about money.

Our couples small group read *The Good Fight*. We'd never been more energized and excited to get to group. Truly, each chapter reveals practical applications that we'd never considered.

The Good Fight showed us what we are REALLY fighting about. That insight has done more than just about anything to curb our conflict.

THE GOOD FIGHT

THE
GOOD
FIGHT

HOW CONFLICT CAN BRING YOU CLOSER

Drs. Les & Leslie Parrott

#1 *NEW YORK TIMES* BEST-SELLING AUTHORS

WORTHY®
PUBLISHING

Published by Worthy Publishing, a division of Worthy Media, Inc., One Franklin Park, 6100 Tower Circle, Suite 210, Franklin, TN 37067.

HELPING PEOPLE EXPERIENCE THE HEART OF GOD

eBook available at worthypublishing.com

Audio book distributed through Brilliance Audio, visit brillianceaudio.com

Library of Congress Control Number: 2012956461

For foreign and subsidiary rights, contact Riggins International Rights, Inc.; rigginsrights.com.

Published in association with Yates & Yates, yates2.com

ISBN: 978-1-61795-661-4 (Trade Paper)

Cover Design: Kent Jensen, Knail LLC, knail.com
Cover Image: Brandon Hill, Brandon Hill Photos, brandonhillphotos.com
Interior Design and Typesetting: Kristi C Smith, Juicebox Designs, juiceboxdesigns.com

Printed in the United States of America
17 18 19 LBM 9 8 7

To Scott and Theresa—
a couple doing more to help other couples
fight a good fight than most will ever know.

★ CONTENTS ★

★ ACKNOWLEDGMENTS ★

WORTHY PUBLISHING LIVES UP to its name. Byron Williamson, president and publisher, caught the vision for this book from the moment we first mentioned it. So did Jeana Ledbetter, our editorial expert. Jennifer Day and Tom Williams polished every sentence. And the sales, marketing, and publicity team are some of the best in the business: Dennis Disney, Morgan Canclini, Alyson White, Betty Woodmancy, and Sherrie Slopianka. We could not be more grateful to the entire Worthy family for allowing us to publish with them.

We owe a special debt to a handful of couples who literally read aloud an early draft of this book in a single sitting together. They traveled from around the country to do this for us, and each of them added immeasurable value to the project. Ranjy and Shine Thomas are two of the most creative, talented, and giving people we know (and we have the late night phone records to prove it). Brandon and Kristin Hill have endured Sunday brunches after church to help us unpack our thinking on this book. And it's also Brandon who talked us into an arm-wrestling match—which he photographed for the book's cover. Rich and Linda Simmons offered sage advice and wisdom at multiple turns. And Tim and Beth Popadic, flying to Seattle from Palm Beach, Florida, have gone way beyond the extra mile to invest in the message of this book with us. In fact, it was Tim, with his trademark mojo, who fanned a flame for live Fight Night events with us in cities across the country.

A band of people in Boulder, Colorado, have also invested themselves in this project. We're deeply grateful to our Rocky Mountain friends: Ryan Holdeman, Sara Meyer, Jeff Fray, Bob Brown, Brian McKinney, Caleb Hanson, Leora Weiner, Tory Leggat, Mark Ferguson, Brian Ledbetter, Ryan DeCook, Justin VanEaton, Liz Swanson, and Eric Swanson.

Dr. John Gottman has done more yeoman's work on the empirical side of understanding couples conflicts than anyone we know. And in a sense, the seeds of this book were first planted many years ago over a delightful lunch we had with John overlooking Lake Washington. Throughout the writing of this book we've stood on his shoulders.

Finally, we want to thank five very important people in our lives. Sealy Yates is not only a great comrade in publishing but a great friend. Mandi Moragne, our director of Amazing Customer Experiences, cares about the people we serve every bit as much as we do. Janice Lundquist has managed our life on the road (and more) in a way that two travelers have no right to expect or ask. Kevin Small, the chair of our nonprofit, is incredibly helpful at every turn. And Ryan Farmer, along with his wife, Kendra, are unimaginable gifts to our efforts. Ryan adds value to everything he touches, and we could not be more grateful to him and our entire team who have worked so hard on our behalf. We can't say thanks enough.

★ A SPECIAL NOTE ABOUT THE APP ★
IT'S POWERFUL, FUN, AND FREE!

GET *THE GOOD FIGHT* for iPhone or Android for free (valued at $12). In it you'll find videos, assessments, games, and more that will help you personalize the content of this book.

It contains more than two dozen applets that relate specifically to what you will read in this book, and it will help you to put it into practice.

As you're reading along, you will occasionally encounter a box that looks like this:

THE GOOD FIGHT

This app is like nothing you've seen before. It's designed exclusively with the two of you in mind. And it's chock-full of helpful tools geared to bring the two of you closer. It contains several short videos from us as well as self-tests, exercises, games, and more.

This app creates the world's smallest social network—the two of you. And it's private. And if you purchased this book, it's free.

As far as we know, this is the first book to provide such a powerful and useful tool. We think you're going to love it. As you'll soon see, you can communicate with us along the way, if you choose, right from the app. We'll reply promptly. We hope to hear from you soon!

To get *The Good Fight* on your smartphone, visit **www.GoodFight.us** and use the code below:

CXE2J36

★ INTRODUCTION ★
WHEN THE FUR FLIES

Marriage is one long conversation,
checkered with disputes.
ROBERT LOUIS STEVENSON

"HOW MANY OF YOU have ever struggled with conflict in your relationship?" It's a question Leslie and I often ask couples during our marriage seminars.

The majority of hands shoot up without hesitation.

"Keep your hands up," I tell them. "Look around. Do you see the people who aren't holding up their hands? What do we call them?"

The audience replies in unison: "Liars!"

It's true. No couple, no matter how loving, is immune to conflict. It's inevitable. Recent research reveals that the average married couple argues about small, nagging things as much as 312 times per year.[1] That means most couples experience a tug-of-war of some kind on a near-daily basis. It doesn't mean they don proverbial boxing gloves and step into the ring for a major bout. It just means that conflicts in marriage— the little scrapes, spats, and squabbles—are endemic.

Even as married professionals—a psychologist (Les) and a marriage and family therapist (Leslie)—we have our fair share of tussles. We're the first to admit it. In fact, we had one of our worst fights just before we were about to speak on the art of love to an auditorium of eager couples (more on that later). The point is, if you're in a relationship, you've got to learn to fight it out fairly.

LOVE AND WAR

A few years ago, while traveling in China, we were invited into the humble home of an elderly couple outside of Beijing. Through an interpreter, Les commented on the bright red paper decorations around the small doorframe of the otherwise drab two-room home. This delighted the eighty-something husband and wife who lived there.

As they invited us in, our hosts bowed repeatedly and directed us to a wooden table that looked about as old as they were. The home was dimly lit by a single exposed lightbulb. It was hot and humid. The air was stagnant and stale. They offered us handheld fans, which we gladly accepted. Speaking only a few words of English, they demonstrated the ancient art of *jianzhi*, Chinese paper cutting. Soon they gave each of us a pair of surprisingly modern scissors and a sheet of bright red paper, asking us to follow their directions. We carefully folded and cut the red paper as our hosts directed us. After dozens and dozens of intricate, precise cuts, we unfolded our work.

> Conflict is inevitable, but combat is optional.
> MAX LUCADO

"What is it?" Les asked.

"It is a special symbol," our hosts replied through the interpreter. "It is used only at weddings. It symbolizes 'double happiness.'"

As we examined our work, we engaged in some lighthearted teasing between us about which of us had done a better job of creasing and cutting the paper. Our hosts, knowing little English, thought we were having a tiff until our interpreter explained our playful banter, letting them know we were just having fun.

"Your hosts want you to know," said the interpreter, "that we have a saying in China: 'Even the teeth sometimes bite the tongue.'"

Before we could ask for an explanation, the couple giggled in delight. This wise husband then said, "Even loving couple have war."

We all laughed. The spirit of his message was clear. He was stating a marriage truth that transcends oceans and national boundaries: even in the closest and most loving of relationships, we sometimes have painful moments when "the teeth bite the tongue."

Conflict. It's pervasive, recurring, and universal.

ALLIES, NOT ADVERSARIES

Just because two people argue doesn't mean they don't love each other. Just because they don't argue doesn't mean they do. In fact, generally speaking, couples who supposedly never fight are either redefining fighting to make them immune or are walking on eggshells to avoid telling each other the truth. We'll say it again: all couples fight. Fighting is as intrinsic to marriage as sex. And the goal for both activities is to do them well.

As you are about to see in this first chapter, what matters is *how* we fight, not *whether* we fight. It's how we fight—the quality of our quarreling—that determines the closeness of our relationship. Multiple studies have identified what separates happy from not-so-happy couples. One answer surfaces every time. Happy couples have a lock on healthy conflict resolution. They know how to fight well. Couples who stay happily married disagree just as much as couples who get divorced, but they have learned how to use those disagreements to deepen their connection. They've built a bridge over issues that would otherwise divide them. Above all, happily married couples see each other as allies, not adversaries.

READY TO RUMBLE?

We hope you've downloaded the app. If not, you'll want to do so now by going to www.GoodFight.us. The *Ready to Rumble* applet will give you a fun overview of *The Good Fight* and show you how to take full advantage of what you are about to experience in this book.

WHY WE WROTE THIS BOOK

In a *New York Times* interview focusing on her thirty-plus-year marriage, Anne Meara of the comedy team Stiller and Meara was asked, "Was it love at first sight?" "It wasn't then," she replied, "but it sure is now."[2]

That sentiment gets at our intentions for writing this book. We're a living example of how learning to fight a good fight can bring a husband and wife closer together. Over the years, we've written books for couples about communication, sex, empathy, parenting, spirituality, time management, and personality, but never a book about conflict. We wanted to get it right first. So with over twenty-five years to practice what we preach in this book, we're ready and eager to show you what we've learned.

Everything in this book—every tip and tool—has been time-tested in our own relationship and with countless couples just like you. You won't find flippant platitudes, silly strategies, and hackneyed advice here. We're giving you innovative and sometimes counterintuitive approaches that work.

If you are feeling especially entrenched in conflict that seems almost impossible to change or overcome, we want you to know there is reason for optimism. You might be thinking you are doomed to a relationship of strife. Maybe you've swallowed as truth the old proverb that "As you have made your bed, so you must lie in it." Don't buy that lie. That's ridiculous. You don't have to put up with a belligerent bed. As G. K. Chesterton said, "If I have made my bed uncomfortable, please God, I will make it again." You can remake your marriage by learning to fight a good fight.

Whether you fight a little or a lot, this book is for you. Whether you are dating, engaged, newly married, or married for decades, this book is for you. If you're tired of squabbles, quarrels, tiffs, and conflicts that assault your love life—or if you just want to ensure that they don't—this book is for you. In these pages you will find practical help for turning those tiresome moments into milestones that mark deeper intimacy and greater passion for each other. This book is for every couple who wants their relationship to be "love at first sight" now.

> Marriage is nature's way of keeping us from fighting with strangers.
> ALAN KING

— Drs. Les and Leslie Parrott
Seattle, Washington

THE GOOD FIGHT INVENTORY

GOOD
FIGHT

Before you begin the next chapter you may want to take just five minutes or so to complete a little self-test. *The Good Fight Inventory* will help you capture your personal perspective on conflict. It will give you the "big picture" when it comes to conflict in your relationship. But don't worry. It won't diagnose you. It's primary purpose is to get your wheels spinning.

★ CHAPTER 1 ★

WHAT MOST COUPLES DON'T KNOW ABOUT CONFLICT

No pressure, no diamonds.
MARY CASE

WE HAD JUST COMPLETED two days of speaking to an exuberant group of couples in the southeast end of London. The venue was only two blocks from the famed Abbey Road Studios where tourists take countless photos of themselves walking over the zebra crossing to replicate the cover of the Beatles' 1969 *Abbey Road* album.

Following our seminar, we ambled over to the crossing and did our own imitations of Paul and Ringo. We had the time because we were staying over a couple of days to celebrate our wedding anniversary. Our boys were safe at home in Seattle with their grandmother, so we were footloose and carefree—just the two of us.

Wedding anniversaries are big occasions with us, so we splurged shamelessly. A nice hotel, a leisurely brunch after waking without an alarm clock, window-shopping on Oxford Street, high tea at Fortnum & Mason in the afternoon, a dinner of prime rib and Yorkshire pudding and cherries jubilee that night at the Savoy Grill. Then, under a clear night sky, we strolled hand-in-hand along Westminster Bridge while taking in the majesty of Big Ben, London's iconic landmark. Extravagant? Luxurious? Delicious? Romantic? Yes, all of the above. The entire experience was idyllic—one for the memory books.

And then, suddenly, without warning, it happened.

"I want to buy a couple of sweatshirts for the boys," Leslie said.

"Um, hmm," I replied, watching people hop onto the back of a bus. "Why don't we have double-decker buses in Seattle?"

"Did you hear me?" Leslie said a bit sternly.

"Sure. You want to buy something for the boys."

"Do you remember where we saw those red ones near the hotel?"

"They're all over the place," I said, pointing to a line of red buses.

"I'm talking about sweatshirts," said Leslie. "Do you think they'd still be open this late?"

"I'm pretty sure we can't fit two big sweatshirts into our suitcase. Besides, do you think they really need more sweatshirts?"

Sensing she was going to have to argue a strong case for buying the sweatshirts, Leslie replied with an edge in her voice, "I'm not going home without something for the boys."

> Empathy is the great unsung human gift.
> JEAN BAKER MILLER

"Fine," I replied, thinking we could still steer this conversation away from the brink. "How about something easier to pack?"

"They love those hooded sweat-shirts. Are you going to help me find them or not?" Leslie abruptly unfolded a map of the city.

"I'm just saying—"

"I know what you're saying!"

"Oh, really?" I said with a caustic tone. "What am I saying?"

Leslie, having found something on the map—or just pretending she had—started to walk quickly, a couple of paces in front of me, without saying anything.

"Why are you walking so fast?" I asked as if I didn't know.

"Angry energy," she snapped without skipping a beat.

"Angry energy?" I asked with genuine intrigue and a little grin in my voice. It was a pretty astute comment for someone so perturbed.

She didn't answer. We walked in silence for a few paces, Leslie marching two steps ahead of me.

At the end of the block, waiting for a traffic signal to change, she said, "Maybe we should stop in there for a while." She pointed to a sign on an historic building: Cabinet War Rooms.

I smiled.

She smiled back.

That was it.

We found a turning point. The icy tension of our brief spat was about to thaw. Without saying another word, we held hands again and kept walking the better part of the block. The pressure was off, but we needed a moment to let our hearts recalibrate.

After a few more strides, Leslie squeezed my hand to say she was with me. I got the message and squeezed back.

We came to Downing Street. "Shall we see if the prime minister is in?" I asked.

"He's probably managing an international conflict somewhere," she said, knowing she was lobbing me an easy one.

"Or maybe one with his wife," I quipped.

We walked a few more steps and turned the corner, literally and metaphorically.

"We did a nice job there," Leslie said, still holding my hand.

I knew exactly what she meant.

We were quietly congratulating ourselves on putting the kibosh on what could have become a full-fledged fight. In spite of the flare-up, we were still an "us." We'd staved off a quarrel that was looking to come between us. We'd turned around our tiny tiff in just a few moments, and we knew we were stronger because of it. Early in our marriage, the same kind of quarrel could have snowballed into a brawl that would have spoiled the whole trip. One of us would have resorted to fighting dirty, sabotaging the solution with sanctimonious blame or upping the ante by sniping at the other's character.

Not now. We've gotten wise to the ways of the marital street fight. We've learned to cut it down before it cuts us up. No blood. No scars. Not even a scratch. We've learned a better way that actually draws us closer. In short, we've learned the difference between fighting with honor and fighting without it. The former is always better.

A CONVERSATIONAL AUTOPSY

We all know that conflict has the potential to inflict hurt, resentment, and stress. It can escalate hostility and rob couples of valuable time and energy. It depletes intimacy and pulls otherwise loving couples apart.

Our little spat in London was primed to do exactly that. We were doing fine one moment, but in a flash we were at odds with each other. How could that happen? We were enjoying what was surely one of the best days we could ever dream of, and suddenly, out of nowhere, we were sideswiped by a silly squabble neither of us saw coming.

Over the years we've done enough postmortems on our potential fights that we've come to call the practice a "conversational autopsy." Here's how each of us sized up this one:

> *Leslie:* From my perspective, Les didn't know that, as the evening grew later, a problem was dawning on me: I was

about to run out of time to get something nice for our boys. Not only that, they both needed a sweatshirt for the start of school, and I knew they'd love the ones I'd seen in a shop window earlier. I hadn't mentioned this to Les, so it wasn't on his radar. It wasn't fair for me to expect him to know of my concern. But that's not all. Les didn't know I was about five days premenstrual. At the time, that fact didn't register with me either.

Les: From my perspective, I was surprised that Leslie had abruptly become task-oriented when we were just enjoying the relaxing evening. When she said she wasn't going home without getting something for our boys, I felt that she was saying I didn't care about bringing our boys a present they would enjoy. I felt judged. But what she really meant was that she'd already determined what would be best for them and assumed I'd go along with it. Of course, it never dawned on me that her hormones might be contributing to the mix.

All those factors from our perspectives added to the mysterious amalgamation of motives, perceptions, and inferences that created unexpected tension between us. At least, that's the best we can make of it in retrospect. Maybe that's why it happened or maybe not. The bottom line is that these little land mines erupt without notice on a regular basis for every couple. It's a given. What matters is how we deal with them.

> More than any other single deficiency, I think it is the lack of mutual empathy which results in sword-drawing in marriage.
> **BERNARD GUERNEY**

We haven't always known how to deal with our conflicts, and we've had some real humdingers along the way. Like the fight that ensued in our car on a Saturday morning while we were running errands. That one didn't end until the next day. The conflict? It was a circular conversation over who was pulling more weight on the home front. In short, it was a chore war, and each of us had drawn a battle line. We both dug in our heels and were dead set on proving the other person wrong.

"It would be nice if you could actually lend a hand on occasion," Leslie said sardonically.

"Seriously?!" Les retorted. "You're actually going to say I don't help out?"

"Do I need to?"

"Apparently!"

"Okay, then, you *don't* help out."

"What do you want me to do that I'm not doing?" Les asked the question as if Leslie would have to think long and hard to answer it. She didn't.

"How many do you want?

"C'mon."

"Let's start with taking out the trash."

"I do take it out!"

"Then why did we have a heaping pile of rubbish in our garage for the past two weeks?"

"Oh, that's rich! You know I was traveling and—"

"And you didn't take it out before you left."

We jabbered on like this throughout the day, with accusations hopscotching around to various chores: cleaning bathrooms, yard work, and so on. When we weren't talking about it, we were each building up our case and reloading our ammunition for the moment the battle engaged once more. Each of us was far more concerned with winning the fight than resolving it. We were in a serious power struggle, a world-class game of blame, and we were dangerously close to belittling each other with true contempt. In short, we were having an honest-to-goodness bad fight. Except there wasn't anything honest or good about it.

At the time, we didn't really know it was a bad fight, because early in our marriage we didn't know there was a distinction between a good fight and a bad one. We just thought a fight was a fight. But that's far from the truth.

To deal effectively with any conflict, we've got to know the difference between a good fight and a bad fight.

WHEN THE GLOVES COME OFF

Professionals formerly believed that couples who were more prone to arguments were the least satisfied with their marriage. The studies that led to those findings, however, failed to distinguish among the kinds of fights the couples were having.[1] Truth be told, the difference between a marriage that grows happier and one that grows more miserable is not *whether* they fight but *how* they fight.

All fights are not created equal. A good fight, in contrast to a bad fight, is helpful, not hurtful. It is positive, not negative. A good fight stays clean, but a bad fight gets dirty. According to researchers at the University of Utah, 93 percent of couples who fight dirty will be divorced within ten years.[2] A study at Ohio State University showed that unhealthy marital arguments contribute significantly to a higher risk of heart attacks, headaches, back pain, and a whole slew of other health problems, not to mention unhappiness.[3] In the end, bad fights lead to marriages that are barely breathing and will eventually die. In fact, researchers can now predict with 94 percent accuracy

> Respect is a two-way street. If you want to get it, you've got to give it.
> R. G. RISCH

whether or not a couple will stay together based solely on how they fight.[4] Not *whether* they fight, but *how* they fight.

The line separating good fights from bad is not fuzzy. Research makes the difference clear, and the following chart lays it out plainly.

	BAD FIGHT	GOOD FIGHT
GOAL	Winning the fight	Resolving the fight
TOPIC	Surface issues	Underlying issues
EMPHASIS	Personalities and power struggles	Ideas and issues
ATTITUDE	Confrontational and defensive	Cooperative and receptive
MOTIVATION	Shift blame	Take responsibility
MODE	Belittle	Respect
MANNER	Egocentric	Empathic
DEMEANOR	Self-righteous	Understanding
SIDE EFFECT	Escalation of tension	Easing of tension
RESULT	Discord	Harmony
BENEFIT	Stagnation and distance	Growth and intimacy

Arguments where one partner or the other becomes defensive or stubborn or withdraws are particularly destructive. Belittling and blame are also toxic. The list of qualities that make up a bad fight could go on and on, but if you boil the essence of a bad fight down to a single ingredient and sum it all up in a word, it would have to be *pride*.

PRIDE FIGHTING

In the book *Love in the Time of Cholera*, Nobel laureate Gabriel García Márquez portrays a marriage that disintegrates over a bar of soap. It was the wife's job to keep the house in order, including the towels, toilet paper, and soap in the bathroom. One day she forgot to replace the soap. Her husband exaggerated the oversight: "I've been bathing for almost a week without any soap." Although she had indeed forgotten, she vigorously denied forgetting to replace the soap. Her pride was at stake, and she would not back down. For the next seven months they slept in separate rooms and ate in silence. Their marriage suffered a meltdown.

"Even when they were old and placid," writes Márquez, "they were very careful about bringing it up, for the barely healed wounds could begin to bleed again as if they had been inflicted only yesterday." How can a bar of soap ruin a marriage? The answer is simple: pride. Both husband and wife were hanging on to it with a vise grip. The husband wouldn't overlook an offense; the wife wouldn't admit a mistake. Both refused to let go of their need to win, to show the other that they were superior.

> Love is honesty. Love is a mutual respect for one another.
> SIMONE ELKELES

The Bible makes it plain: "Pride leads to conflict."[5] It's that simple. A prideful spirit keeps us from cooperating, flexing, respecting, compromising, and resolving. Instead, it fuels defensiveness and discord.[6] It stands in the way of saying "I'm sorry." It lives by the motto "The only unfair fight is the one you lose." Self-centered pride is at the heart of every bad fight.

Research shows that when pride sets in, a partner will continue an argument 34 percent of the time even if he knows he's wrong or can't remember what the fight was about. A full 74 percent will fight on even if they feel "it's a losing battle."[7]

Let's be clear: healthy pride (the pleasant emotion of being pleased by our work) is quite different from unhealthy pridefulness in which our egos are bloated. The latter is laced with arrogance and conceit. That's what we're talking about here.

We don't have to be egomaniacs to suffer from unhealthy pride. It
has a way of secretly seeping into the crevices of our conflicts even when
we are consciously inclined to avoid it. That's what makes it so toxic and
devious. "Through pride we are ever deceiving ourselves," said Carl
Jung. "But deep down below the surface of the average conscience a
still, small voice says to us, something is out of tune."

You know the feeling of being out of tune. We all do. It's born of the
tension between being the kind of person we want to be and our fear of
being snookered. We don't want to be prideful, but we also don't want
to be duped. The tension be-
tween those two concerns is
what causes pride to kick in.
That's when we realize, deep
down, that we've taken the
low road. More often than not, this sinking feeling even becomes more
difficult to admit to ourselves, let alone our spouse, so we accede to our
pride and perpetuate the conflict.

> Reverence reduces hostility.
> **TOBA BETA**

The antidote to unhealthy pride is, of course, humility. The word
from which we get *humility* literally means "from the earth." In other
words, humility steps off its high horse to stand on the earth—to
become common and lowly. Humility isn't for cowards. It's risky.
Humility makes us vulnerable to being played or to being made to look
the fool. But it also makes possible everything else we truly want to be.
Seventeenth-century British author William Gurnall said, "Humility is
the necessary veil to all other graces." Without humility, it's nearly impossible to engender kindness and warmth with our spouse. Without
humility, it's impossible to fight a good fight, the kind that brings you
closer together.

THE PRIDE-O-METER

With this handy tool on your smartphone or tablet, it will take you less than thirty seconds to get a reading on your level of pride at any moment. You'll soon see how this quick increase in self-awareness will help you cultivate more humility, making a good fight far more likely. It's quick and painless. Try it right now.

THE ANATOMY OF A GOOD FIGHT

The cornerstone of every physician's education is anatomy. The word *anatomy* dates back to at least 1600 BC, and it literally means "to open up." Without having opened up human bodies to gain an understanding of human anatomy, it would be impossible for doctors to practice good medicine. In the same way, couples cannot practice good fighting until we understand the substance of a good fight. We need to open it up and see what it's made of.

The following is not an exhaustive list of what makes up a good fight, but it's a look at four critical elements—the central, innermost essentials. They are easy to remember because their initials form an acronym that spells **CORE**: Cooperation, Ownership, Respect, and Empathy.

Cooperation: Good Fighters Fight for a Win-Win

A study reported in *Psychological Science* discovered that, when it comes to couples, the best arguers are those who work in tandem with their partner. According to the study, the person who says "we" the most during an argument suggests the best solutions. The study cited researchers from the University of Pennsylvania and the University of North Carolina at Chapel Hill who used statistical analysis to study 59 couples. Spouses who used second-person pronouns (you) tended toward negativity in interactions. Those making use of first-person plural pronouns (we) provided positive solutions to problems.

The study concluded: "'We'-users may have a sense of shared interest that sparks compromise and other ideas pleasing to both partners. 'You'-sayers, on the contrary, tend to criticize, disagree, justify, and otherwise team with negativity."[8]

How do you cultivate a cooperative spirit when a conflict heats up? It can be a challenge. The good news is that cooperation is a skill set; that is, it can be learned. The more you practice it, the easier it gets. The key to cooperation is found in reframing a conflict from win-lose to win-win. Your conflict is not a competition. Your marriage is not a zero-sum game. Win-win is a frame of mind and heart that seeks mutual benefit. It's an attitude that says, "If you win, I win too." It's committed to finding solutions that benefit both sides of a dispute. There's a sense of "we" in win-win.

> Without honor, all the marriage skills one can learn won't work.
> JOHN GOTTMAN

But let's be honest: not every dispute has a solution for both sides. On a bulletin board in our kitchen is a cartoon of a cat and a dog standing in front of a judge's bench. The dog says, "Let's agree to disagree." When a win-win can't be found, it's time to do just that: agree to disagree.

The phrase first appeared in print in 1770 when English theologian John Wesley wrote a memorial for his friend and colleague George Whitfield. They had doctrinal differences and neither wavered from them, but, as Wesley said, they held fast to the essentials together. In other words, their friendship continued in spite of issues on which they did not agree. It's that kind of attitude, when shared by husband and wife, that creates a win-win for a couple even when they continue to disagree.

GETTING TO WIN-WIN

Ready for a little fun? *Getting to Win-Win* on your smartphone or tablet presents a game that can be won only when the two of you are working together. It's a real-life example of putting into practice what you just read. Not only that, it provides further helps in cultivating more cooperation when the relational tension mounts. In short, this helps you move from a win-lose scenario in your conflicts to seeing more clearly than ever that your conflicts can bring you closer together when you stay on the same team.

Ownership: Good Fighters Own Their Piece of the Pie

Maybe you've seen the bumper sticker "The man who can smile when things are going badly has just thought of someone to blame it on." Sadly, this is sometimes much too close to the truth when it comes to conflict and couples. It's so tempting to play the blame game. Why? Because we think it will let us off the hook. So we say things like

- We wouldn't be in this mess if you knew how to manage our money.
- You're the one who's angry! Not me.
- If you were ever on time, we wouldn't have missed dinner.

When we blame our spouse (or anything else), we shift responsibility. We think our fancy footwork puts us in the clear. Of course, it doesn't work that way. Blame only exacerbates a conflict. In the boxing ring they call it blocking when you twist your shoulders to prevent an opponent's punch from landing squarely on your torso. In a relationship we call it an excuse: "I didn't see the bills until just now."

If we don't try to block the blame with an excuse, we might throw a counterpunch: "Oh, really? So *I'm* the one who doesn't know how to

manage our money? Let's talk about your shopping spree last weekend."
A bout like this can go on and on, until one person quits pointing fingers and takes ownership.

In the final film of the classic boxing series *Rocky*, an aging Rocky Balboa says to his son, "You gotta be willing to take the hits and not point fingers, saying you ain't where you wanna be because of him or her or anybody! Cowards do that, and that's not you!"

The blame game is for cowards. Ownership takes courage. It takes mettle not to be a victim. Shifting blame immediately makes you powerless. But when you take ownership for your piece of the conflict pie, you're instantly empowered to find a solution together.

You say things like

- **It's unfair for me to think you could balance the books with the week you've had.**
- **I admit that I'm feeling angry here, and I don't know what to do.**
- **I didn't think about the traffic when I scheduled the dinner. That was a mistake.**

These are the words of ownership. They drive blame back to its corner.

When Andy Stanley was doing marriage counseling as pastor of his now megachurch in Atlanta, he would get a pad of paper, draw a circle on it, and say to a couple in conflict, "This is a pie that represents all the chaos in your marriage. Now, 100 percent of the blame is in that pie, because that's where all the chaos is." He would give each spouse a pen and say, "I want you to draw a slice of pie that you think represents your responsibility for the chaos."

Are you able to do that? It's tough. It's scary. We humans abhor the vulnerability that comes from taking responsibility. Admitting our imperfections, mistakes, or neediness opens us up to being critiqued, and we'd much rather find someone or something to blame. Admitting any weakness, any mistake, we think, makes us vulnerable to rejection. And it does. That's the risk of taking ownership. That's why a good fight isn't for cowards.

We'd all do well to take some sage advice from poet Ogden Nash:

> *To keep your marriage brimming*
>
> *With love in the loving cup,*
>
> *Whenever you're wrong, admit it;*
>
> *Whenever you're right, shut up.*

OWNING THE CHAOS PIE

Wouldn't it be great to have a tangible way to show how much responsibility we're willing to own (or not own) in the chaos of a particular conflict? This simple clarification can go a long way in helping us quit the blame game so we can get on with the more productive ways of resolving tension. *Owning the Chaos Pie* on your smartphone or tablet reveals—quite literally— how many slices of responsibility you're each willing to own.

Respect: Good Fighters Steer Clear of Belittling

A few steps from our offices on the campus of Seattle Pacific University, you can cross a canal that joins Puget Sound to Lake Washington and walk down a trail to the University of Washington. Some

> Confrontation should always leave a person's dignity intact.
> A. J. ANGLIN

of the most groundbreaking research on marriage ever attempted has been conducted on this campus. In 1986, John Gottman founded a research laboratory with funding from the National Institute of Mental Health where he used video, heart-rate monitors, and measures of pulse amplitude to code the behavior and physiology of hundreds of couples at different points in their relationship. He's done more yeomen's work on conflict in marriage than anyone we know. Over lunch one day, we asked John what single quality was most detrimental to a couple's well-being.

"Contempt," he said, without thinking twice. "Contempt is so lethal to love that it ought to be outlawed." He went on to tell us how predictive contempt is of marital turmoil and even of eventual divorce. Contempt is any belittling remark that makes your spouse feel about an inch tall. It's often sarcastic: "Way to go, Einstein. You're a regular genius." In fact, it doesn't even have to be spoken. Dr. Gottman told us that even eye rolling can be toxic. Contempt conveys disdain, disapproval, and dishonor. In short, contempt conveys disrespect. It sabotages a core element of a good fight.

> I can win an argument on any topic, against any opponent. People know this and steer clear of me at parties. Often, as a sign of their great respect, they don't even invite me.
>
> DAVE BARRY

Everyone wants respect. Scratch that. Everyone *needs* respect. We can't have a relationship without it. An attitude of respect builds a bridge of trust between husband and wife even when they are feeling at odds. Respect does more than curb contempt, however. It helps us to listen before speaking. It drives us to understand before passing judgment.

Both of our boys, somewhere in elementary school, wanted to learn martial arts. We signed them up for karate classes. As we watched from the sidelines of the practice room (the dojo), we were impressed by the instructor's first lesson. He told the boys that every practice and every sparring bout begins and ends with a bow. "It's a sign of respect for your opponent," he told them. That's not a bad life lesson. Respect, even for a challenger, is honorable and good.

Respect keeps contempt at bay, and it also creates safety within the relationship. To paraphrase Benjamin Franklin, respect ensures that even when we don't say the right thing, we leave unsaid the wrong thing at the tempting moment. That's why respect is essential to fighting a good fight.

R-E-S-P-E-C-T

Let's be honest. Nobody wants to think of him- or herself in a bad light. But if we are truthful, most of us know that in the heat of conflict we can sometimes be downright disrespectful or even contemptuous toward our partner. *R-E-S-P-E-C-T* on your smartphone or applet will help you and your partner reduce belittling and increase respect while having a little fun in the process. See if you can find the pictures that best capture your dark side. What photos best depict how you'd like to be shown respect from your partner? This applet is all about the visuals.

Empathy: Good Fighters Step into Each Other's Shoes

For years we have traveled North America and beyond, doing marriage seminars for couples. At some point in nearly every seminar, we tell our audience that if we could press a magic button to improve their relationships instantly, it would be a button that gives them an abundance of empathy. Why empathy? Because empathy, that ability to see accurately the world from your partner's perspective, is the most powerful, consistently rewarding action of love you can ever take. Unfortunately, empathy is in far too short supply when couples are conflicting.

Have you ever said anything like

- I simply don't understand him.
- I have no idea what would make her happy.
- We'll just be talking, and he blows up for no reason.
- I don't understand why she keeps bringing this up.

Each statement reveals a lack of understanding, a lack of empathy. But hear this: if you want to instantly and dramatically increase the odds of experiencing a good fight, you may only need to put the single core quality of empathy into practice. Why? Because research shows that 90 percent of marital spats can be resolved if all the couple does is accurately see the issue from each other's perspective. Don't miss this point: nine times out of ten, conflicts are resolved when couples step into each other's shoes.

We call it trading places, and we've witnessed its simple power with numerous couples. On one occasion we accompanied a warring couple to a shopping mall. They repeatedly fought over money. He was a spender; she was a saver. Neither could see money from the other's point of view—until we had them trade places. We had them walk into a department store and do their best to think, act, and talk like the other person. The wife immediately sat down in a chair that was on sale and said, "We've got to buy this."

"Oh, now, honey," the husband responded, "we don't have money for that."

"But it's on sale," she continued.

"If it's on sale now, it will be on sale later."

Each took on the other's persona with surprising ease. And the result? After a few minutes, they were both laughing about the experience. They had entered each other's world for the first time, and soon each began to explore the other's world. They talked about how differently each of them was raised concerning money matters. They talked about what money symbolized personally for them. Without any prodding from us, they even talked about what they could do to get on the same financial page in order to diminish the tension.

That's the power of empathy.

TRADING PLACES

What would happen if you became your partner for the next twenty-four hours? What if you were to step into his or her shoes, live in the other's skin, and see the world as your mate does? How would your day be different? Would you feel more secure walking down the street or less? Would you feel more responsible or less? *Trading Places* **will help you answer these questions by helping you walk through a typical day in your partner's shoes. It's a fast track to empathy. Warning: You just might never look at each other the same way again. And that's a good thing.**

There you have it. The **CORE** of a good fight is comprised of Cooperation, Ownership, Respect, and Empathy. When you get a lock on these qualities, your fighting will never be the same. In fact, as you are about to see, you'll reap the rewards that only two good fighters enjoy.

FOR REFLECTION

- Review the chart in this chapter that draws a line between good fights and bad fights. Then think of the last few conflicts you've experienced. If you were to put yourself on one side of that line or the other, where would you stand on each of the qualities listed?

- Do you agree that pride is at the center of a bad fight? Why or why not? Can you identify an example of how pride fueled a bad fight in your own life? What happened? How would it have been different if pride had not been present?

- When you consider the **CORE** of a good fight (**C**ooperation, **O**wnership, **R**espect, and **E**mpathy), which of the four elements comes easiest to you? Which is toughest for you to demonstrate? Why?

CHAPTER 2

THE SURPRISING BENEFITS OF A GOOD FIGHT

The greatest of all faults, I should say,
is to be conscious of none.
THOMAS CARLYLE

LET'S START OFF WITH a big benefit that comes from learning to fight well: research shows that couples who learn how to argue productively, compared to couples who do not, cut their chances of divorce in half.[1] Not bad, right? In fact, if that were the only benefit to learning the rudiments of a good fight, it would be enough. After all, we all want our love to go the distance. But fighting right brings even more payoffs. Healthy fighting not only keeps us together, it makes our marriage better on numerous counts. Let's look at some of these other benefits.

AUTHENTICITY: A GOOD FIGHT KEEPS US REAL

"Marriage does not so much bring you into confrontation with your spouse, as to confront you with yourself," says Tim Keller, founding pastor of Redeemer Presbyterian Church in New York City. Isn't that the truth?

Marriage is the closest bond possible between two people. Legally, socially, emotionally, and physically, there is no other means of getting closer to another human being. It is the desire for this extraordinary closeness that propels us into matrimony. We long to belong to another person who knows us and loves us like nobody else in the world. This kind of intimacy is the rocket fuel of marriage. Without intimacy, life becomes horribly cold and lonely. So we plunge ourselves into marriage and give our heart in exchange for the heart of another to discover the deepest and most radical expression of human connection possible.

Eventually, however, couples also discover that such closeness creates confrontation. Why? Because marriage comes with a built-in mirror. Your spouse, by default, becomes a full-time observer of your life, and you become the same for your spouse. We bear witness to nearly everything the other says or does. We begin seeing, in both the other and ourselves, our behaviors, attitudes, and motivations like never before. We give and receive feedback, invited or not, that can rub us the wrong way. But this interchange also makes us better. It heightens our self-awareness and makes us more congruent, more authentic.

> If we manage conflict constructively, we harness its energy for creativity and development.
> **KENNETH KAYE**

Authenticity occurs when our thoughts, words, feelings, and actions come into alignment. Within the intimacy of marriage, we cannot as easily get away with believing we're one way when, in fact, we're actually another. At least not when we are secure enough to be honest and willing to seek and speak the truth.

But even in the most loving of relationships, truth telling can cause conflict. "By marrying," Robert Louis Stevenson warned, "you have willfully introduced a witness into your life . . . and can no longer close the mind's eye upon uncomely passages, but must stand up straight and put a name upon your actions."[3] Why? Because if you don't, your partner will.

A husband is talking on the phone, and when he hangs up, his wife comes in and says, "Did I just hear you take credit for organizing that volunteer effort? I thought Amy did all the work." A simple question like that from his live-in monitor should cause him to reflect on his behavior. But his need for honesty is not likely to be his first reaction, is it? He is likely to be offended that his integrity is being questioned. He might get angry that his wife was eavesdropping on a conversation. But whatever he does, there's likely to be a squabble. He's been cornered, and his fight instinct kicks in.

If, however, during the squabble he has the good sense to lay aside his pride and see his lapse of honesty, he'll come out of it with more integrity, more congruence. Knowing we have this built-in monitor of our words and actions should do much to keep our words and actions aligned with truth.

When your partner says you came across brusquely to a server at a restaurant or questions your motives for disciplining your child, he is causing you to confront yourself—the part of yourself you'd rather avoid. Sure, it may cause tension. It may spur a scuffle. But when you fight well, it also helps you shed pretenses and dishonesty. A good fight keeps you and your relationship real. The more authentic you are as people, the healthier your relationship will be.

CLARITY: A GOOD FIGHT SHEDS LIGHT

The popular *Shrek* movies tell the story of a large green ogre who falls in love with Princess Fiona. They eventually marry and travel to the castle of Fiona's parents in order for Shrek to receive her father's blessing. The visit does not go well, and Shrek and Fiona begin to fight.

After a disagreement with Fiona's father, Shrek barges into Fiona's chambers and starts throwing their things together. As the newlywed's first crisis unfolds, their voices get louder and louder until they're shouting at each other.

Shrek says, "I told you coming here was a bad idea."

"You could have at least tried to get along with my father," Fiona replies.

"You know, somehow I don't think I was going to get Daddy's blessing even if I did want it."

"Well, do you think it might be nice if somebody asked me what I wanted?"

In a sarcastic tone, Shrek responds, "Sure. Do you want me to pack for you?"

"You're unbelievable," says Fiona. "You're behaving like a . . . a . . ."

"Go ahead and say it!" Shrek challenges her.

"Like an ogre!" Fiona shouts.

Shrek yells, "Well, here's a newsflash for you. Whether your parents like it or not, I am an ogre. And guess what, princess—that's not about to change."

Fiona pauses and takes a deep breath. She composes herself, walks slowly to the door, and opens it. In a gentle tone that invites reconciliation, she simply says, "I've made changes for you, Shrek. Think about that." Then she quietly shuts the door behind her, leans up against it, and begins to cry. Shrek, cut to the heart, walks to the door and hears her crying, leans up against his side of it and sighs.[2]

The sound of a sigh is sometimes the indicator of new insight and deeper understanding. Shrek knew Fiona was right. Up to that point, he hadn't even seen the issue. She'd sacrificed a lot for him, and their skirmish eventually made that clear. A good fight does that. It sheds light on something we hadn't seen before.

Recently, while driving as a family on a special outing, I (Les) made some business calls through our car's speakers. This required Leslie, our two boys, and our dog to be quiet. "I've just got to make this one call," I told the group. But that one call turned into a couple more.

"You realize you've been on the phone for nearly an hour," Leslie said.

I shot her a look that said, "You realize I've taken a day away from the office to do this outing, and I've got to get this little bit of work done."

We left it at that. But later that evening, Leslie told me she thought it was inconsiderate of me to make my business calls in the car during a family outing. "The whole point was to have fun as a family," she said, "and that includes the time it takes getting to the beach."

I pushed back: "It was either make those calls or I wouldn't be able to go." We volleyed back and forth a bit with our own perspectives, and eventually I realized how rude it was to have the whole family cater to my calls. To be honest, I probably would never have realized it was even an issue had Leslie not confronted me.

> Each difficult moment has the potential to open my eyes and open my heart.
> **MYLA KABAT-ZINN**

A good fight sheds new light on everything from how we parent to the way we treat each other to how we save, spend, and give our money. A good fight is often like a searchlight that zeros in on an issue that has been quietly lurking around the landscape of our relationship. Once we discover that issue—often through the illuminating blaze of a good fight—we're able to see it and define it, which puts us in a position to do something about it.

FRESH START: A GOOD FIGHT CLEARS THE AIR

For the first five years of our married life, we lived in Los Angeles while attending graduate school. It was the late 1980s, and the city was sometimes referred to as Smogtown. Smog, a combination of smoke and fog, creates a dirty gauze that shrouds buildings and streetlights. On many days it blotted out the mountains we should have been able to see from our city apartment. It would sometimes cause our eyes and lungs to burn. Johnny Carson routinely joked about the lingering menace of smog on *The Tonight Show.* Smog was as much a symbol of Los Angeles as the Hollywood sign it so often obscured.

But the city's long reign as the country's top air polluter ultimately led to a full assault on smog. The number of unhealthy air quality days in the Los Angeles basin has dropped 85 percent since the 1970s. New York, Houston, Denver, and other cities have been taking notes. These days, when we go back to LA from our home city of Seattle, the difference is palpable. Clean air allows you to breathe deeply and enjoy a higher quality of life.

> All married couples should learn the art of battle as they should learn the art of making love. Good battle is objective and honest—never vicious or cruel. Good battle is healthy and constructive.
>
> **ANN LANDERS**

The same is true in marriage. The pollutants of emotional tension, bitterness, stress, strain, woundedness, bad feelings, pressure, animosity, resentments, and walking on eggshells can choke loving feelings right out of the relationship. Collectively, these irritants become a kind of smog that shrouds your marriage in a malaise of discontent. But a good, healthy fight, where both partners open up their feelings in an environment characterized by Cooperation, Ownership, Respect, and Empathy, clears the air.

Our friend Mitch Temple likens a good fight to a lightning storm on a summer night. Although the lightning itself may be scary, it helps to clean the air. Negatively charged ions produced by the storm attach themselves to pollutants, which fall to the ground. That's why the air smells so clean after a good storm.

The same is true when you deal with disagreements in a healthy way. Conflict, when done right, reduces tension, eradicates animosity, and causes hard feelings to disappear. It removes the smog and makes room for a fresh start. Some of the closest moments a couple can experience often arrive after resolving conflicts.

SECURITY: A GOOD FIGHT MAKES YOU STRONGER

An African proverb says, "Smooth seas do not make skillful sailors." It takes a little turmoil to spur any of us to become really good at something—including our relationship. As we weather tough times together and come out on the other side, we build trust and confidence in our relationship. We find security.

This sounds counterintuitive, but a good fight, as opposed to a bad one, actually makes a couple's relationship more solid. It empowers us. We begin to realize we don't have to be afraid of troubles and tension. We can work it out. We're strong. With new confidence, we say to ourselves, *Our love can stand up when it gets knocked around.*

Research at the University of Washington reveals that couples get angry at each other in a good relationship just as they do in a bad one. But they get angry in a very different way. They see a problem as something like a soccer ball. They kick it around together. They aren't afraid to roll up their sleeves and dig into whatever is troubling them. They don't tiptoe around the issue. They say, with respect for their partner, "This is troubling me and we need to talk about it." They don't freeze with tension. They don't put their guard up. They certainly don't vent their anger. They simply put their issues on the table, speak the truth in love, and do whatever it takes to work it out—even when the issue might cause them to feel utterly incompatible.

After being married fifty-four years to the same person, Billy Graham was asked to reveal his secret to staying in love. He said, "Ruth and I are happily incompatible." They understood how healthy conflict makes you stronger.

Get this: couples who are able to acknowledge their partner's faults while maintaining positive views of their marriage overall experience more stability and satisfaction over time.[3] So much for love being blind! The most successful couples air their grievances. They live in the real world with real complaints. But they do so while placing great value on the relationship.

"I didn't marry you because you were perfect," writes Thornton Wilder in *The Skin of Our Teeth*. "I didn't even marry you because I loved you. I married you because you gave me a promise. That promise made up for your faults. And the promise I gave you made up for mine. Two imperfect people got married and it was the promise that made the marriage. And when our children were growing up, it wasn't a house that protected them; and it wasn't our love that protected them—it was that promise."

The integrity that sticks by that "I do" promise grows sturdier when couples fight a good fight. As they shed light on imperfections and weather conflict together, they enrich their original commitment to each other. "Couples who have healthy fights," says John Gottman, "develop a kind of marital efficacy that makes the marriage stronger as time goes on." Decades earlier, theologian Dietrich Bonhoeffer ex-

> Peace is not the absence of conflict but the presence of creative alternatives for responding to conflict.
> DOROTHY THOMPSON

pressed the same sentiment when writing to a young bride and groom from his prison cell in Nazi Germany: "It is not your love that sustains the marriage, but from now on, the marriage that sustains your love."

The benefits of a good fight truly are marvelous. When you know how to manage conflict in your relationship, you not only double your chances for going the distance . . .

- **You become more true and trustworthy with each other.**
- **You gain more clarity on your issues and what defines you as a couple.**
- **You remove the smog of resentments and clear the air for a fresh start.**
- **You fortify the very promise that secures your relationship.**

Every fight has the potential to be good or bad. The difference is determined by how the two fighters handle conflict. So in the next chapter we get personal and help you discover your own conflict quotient.

FOR REFLECTION

- Think of a time when your spouse pointed out some habit or activity that you knew to be self-indulgent, hurtful in some way, or simply wrong. Were you resentful or grateful at the time? Did it cause you to make a change? Do you think you would have changed without that push?

- Have there been times when you felt that your marriage needed a good fight? You and your mate were on different paths. You were pursuing different goals. You could feel the tension building. Think of such a time in your marriage. When the fight finally came, did it open things up and freshen the air in your marriage? What do you think might have happened if you hadn't had the fight?

- Think of a time in your marriage when you were sure you were absolutely right in something you did, but your spouse was hurt or offended by it. Did the ensuing fight cause you to see your mate's viewpoint more clearly? Maybe even for the first time? If not, or if it took a long time for you to see the other side, is it possible that you may need to work harder on developing a better sense of empathy?

★ CHAPTER 3 ★

WHAT YOU'RE *REALLY* FIGHTING ABOUT

For two people in a marriage to live together day
after day is unquestionably the one miracle
the Vatican has overlooked.
BILL COSBY

PHILIP ROSENTHAL HAD A spat with his wife that ended up on national television for everyone's entertainment. It was definitely entertaining. What were they fighting about? A can opener. We did not actually see Mr. and Mrs. Rosenthal fighting, because their senseless quarrel was played out by another couple, Ray and Debra Barone, the characters Rosenthal created for his sitcom smash *Everybody Loves Raymond.*[1]

The popular show seemed so authentic because Rosenthal and his cocreator, comedian Ray Romano, drew heavily from their own relationships for material. Wars of attrition over household items—a suitcase on the stairs, lotion-enriched tissues, sofa covers—are the daily battles we all fight with love. Who hasn't had a senseless battle over room temperature, toothpaste, the dishwasher, or even a can opener?

In the episode, through a series of flashbacks, Ray and Debra separately tell different family members what each claims transpired over the purchase of a new can opener. Two dramatically different viewpoints emerge.

Here's the story from Ray's perspective. He comes home "in a good mood like usual" and asks Debra about dinner.

"I haven't made you any yet," Debra says sternly. "Can you wait?"

"Fine," says Ray in a cheery tone. "I'll make my own dinner." He whistles a happy tune while looking through the cupboards. "Mmm, tuna fish! Now where's that can opener?"

"It's in the drawer," shouts the clearly perturbed Debra, who is sitting a few feet away with her feet up on the kitchen table.

> When we are listened to, it creates us, makes us unfold and expand.
> KARL MENNINGER

"Righty-o," says Ray as he opens the drawer and picks up the can opener.

"I bought a new one," says Debra.

"Oh, did we need a new can opener?"

"It's better! Okay? It cuts from the sides so there's no sharp edges."

"Okay, let's see how this thing works."

"You put it on the can, you twist the thing, you open the can." Debra rolls her eyes, clearly losing her patience.

"Great! A better can opener."

As Ray opens the can, fluid seeps from it and drips down his arm. He laughs playfully. "Would you look at this?" He tries to strain it with a fork, but most of the tuna falls out.

"Was there something wrong with the other can opener?"

"There's nothing wrong with *this* can opener," shouts Debra.

"No, nothing's wrong, honey. I mean, I would have preferred the tuna on bread," says Raymond good-humoredly, "but it's just as delicious right out of the sink."

"This is the can opener I bought, okay, Ray?" Debra barks as she waves it in front of his face. "Because it's better. It's not stupid. And I'm not stupid!" She throws the can opener into the sink and stalks out of the kitchen.

Ray innocently asks, "What'd I say?"

Of course, Debra sees the entire incident from an entirely different perspective. She recalls Ray's coming home in a grumpy mood and asking about dinner.

"I haven't had time to make you anything yet," Debra says as she's helping their young children. "But if you could just wait."

"Fine," Ray whines. "I'll make my own dinner—again." He pulls a can from the cupboard and sarcastically says, "Mmm, tuna fish. Where's the can opener?"

"It's in the drawer, the utensil drawer."

Ray rummages around in the drawer, making all kinds of racket until Debra comes over to help him.

"Here, I bought a new one."

"Did we need a new can opener?" Ray asks in a judgmental tone.

"It's better. It cuts from the sides so there's no sharp edges." Debra demonstrates how to use it, and when Ray picks up the can, a droplet falls on his finger.

"Tuna juice," he shouts hysterically. "Tuna juice! Was there something wrong with the old can opener?"

"Well, there's nothing wrong with this can opener," Debra explains.

"Oh, no, nothing," Ray says sarcastically.

Debra, starting to tear up, says, "This is the can opener I bought because it was better. It's not stupid and I'm not stupid." She gently sets it on the counter and walks from the room, weeping.

"What'd I say?" Ray asks in a sardonic tone.

So what's the truth? Whose scenario is correct? The answer, of course, is hard to pin down. Both Ray and Debra's answers to that question depend on the differing perception each brings to the event. Both interpret correctness through their unique telling of the situation. The perception of each may be wrong or partly wrong. Or it may even be that one of them is right or more nearly right than the other. Perception does not always determine reality, but it does often lead to conflict.

Understanding perception is vital to managing conflict. Two people often see the same thing differently. "What you see and what you hear depends a great deal on where you are standing," said C. S. Lewis. Our interpretation of a situation is so germane to its potential volatility that we dedicate this chapter to uncovering its power and leveraging our often-contradictory perceptions to our advantage.

First, we want to underscore how our perceptions can lead to misunderstandings and conflict. By analyzing these perceptions, we'll uncover the *real* reason for your fights. You may be surprised to find that your fights are rarely over what they appear to be.

DO YOU SEE WHAT I SEE?

It's Saturday night, and we're going out with friends for a bite to eat. Les is fiddling on his computer when I walk into his study, twirl in front of his desk, and ask, "How do I look?"

Les glances up and says, with little expression, "Fine with me."

I'm not going for "fine with me," so what do you think I did? I walk straight back to my closet in the bedroom and look for a new outfit. A few minutes pass and I hear Les calling, "Where are you? We're going to be late."

As I walk down the stairs, he looks incredulous. "Why did you change your clothes?"

"Because you didn't like what I was wearing."

"I said it was fine with me."

"I heard what you said."

"Okay," he says slowly. "So why the change?"

"What I heard was 'Fine with me. It's your reputation if you want to go out wearing that, so go right ahead.'"

"Such a thought never entered my mind," he insists. "I like what you had on and I was merely distracted by an important email."

Truth be told, I believe him—now. But in that moment I wasn't so sure. I read meaning into his remark whether it was intended or not. My interpretation, my perception, was all I had to go on.

It's difficult to exaggerate the power of perception for couples. Our interpretation of what our spouse says, does, or thinks—whether true or not—can make or break our relationship. It fuels our behavior. It frames our outlook. Perception shapes our attitude as well as our sense of reality. In fact, at any moment, we believe our perception *is* our reality. That's the basis of a great deal of conflict. What one person perceives as reasonable or appropriate, another perceives as unreasonable or inappropriate. That's the nature of perception.

FEATHERS OR FUR?

Almost every college student takes an introductory psychology course, and almost every psychology professor prefers not to teach it. The professors would rather forgo the broad survey of topics with so many freshmen and teach their specialty to upperclassmen who tend to be more serious about their studies. But not me (Les). I

> The person who has understanding has everything.
> JEWISH PROVERB

love teaching the two hundred newcomers in my general psychology class every autumn. I like the challenge of corralling so many minds at the outset of their college career. I especially enjoy the week spent on sensation and perception. For as long as an hour, we look at various illusions projected on the huge screen in the classroom auditorium.

Each illustrates a different way our brain is trained to make sense of something we perceive.

I often start with an easy one, like the following image:

So how about you? What do you see? You might think the question is silly. After all, you clearly see that it's an animal. But not everyone sees the same animal. Some see a duck. Others see a rabbit. I can tell you from experience that whichever one you see first makes it difficult to see the other. But they are both there. One has feathers, the other fur. It all comes down to perception.

You might wonder what this has to do with managing conflict. The answer? Everything. A great percentage of conflicts are not real conflicts at all, but rather a matter of misunderstanding based on perception.

- **A wife asks her husband if he ate the last bit of ice cream, thinking she might serve it to him later that evening. But he perceives the question as an attack. He thinks she is nagging him about his diet. The thought never entered her mind, but that didn't keep the question from flaring into a fight.**
- **A husband asks if his wife is wearing a new dress, thinking it looks great. She interprets the question as his saying she's spending too much money on her wardrobe. The money matter didn't even occur to him. But that didn't prevent a verbal scuffle from ensuing.**

All it takes is one misperception for a couple to go at it. So many marital spats are the result of looking at the same issue from completely different perspectives.

In my psychology course, I have students write down, without talking to their classmates, what they see in the above picture. Then I ask them to raise their hand if they see a duck. About half the hands go up. Same for the rabbit. A few, of course, can see both animals readily. But many struggle to see the other until I tell them the rabbit is looking to the left and the duck is looking up. "Oh, I see it now" is the typical response.

As we progress through the images, they become more difficult to decipher. For example, what do you see here?

I'll give you hint. It's not a duck or rabbit. In fact, even if I tell you what it is, there's a good chance you still won't see it. It's a dog. Right there in plain sight. He's in the center of the picture where we see him from a three-quarter back view, and he's sniffing the ground. Unless you've studied this picture before, you still may struggle to see it. But the dog is there, and once you see him, you can't *not* see him.

The point is this: sometimes you may have no clue about your partner's perception. You just don't see it. Or maybe your mate doesn't see yours. Either way, it leads to frustration and tension. One of you might feel belittled. One of you might feel superior. Either way, your differing perceptions make you more prone to conflict.

At a couples' conference, we saw a brief but humorous sketch that underscores the sometimes absurd nature of our perceptions.

> *Husband:* Change don't come easily.
> *Wife:* Doesn't.
> *Husband:* Doesn't what?
> *Wife:* Come easily. Change *doesn't* come easily.
> *Husband:* So you are agreeing with me.
> *Wife:* Yes, but—
> *Husband:* Then why didn't you just say, "I agree"?
> *Wife:* But I—
> *Husband:* We're always arguing.
> *Wife:* I'm not arguing.
> *Husband:* Yes, you are.
> *Wife:* No, I'm not.
> *Husband:* Then what is it we're doing?
> *Wife:* Honestly, I have no idea.
> *Husband:* Well, whatever it is, I'm sick of it, and it needs to change!
> *Wife:* To quote a wise man, "Change don't come easily."
> *Husband:* Exactly![2]

So many of our conflicts are not real differences at all; they are merely matters of misperception that lead to misunderstanding. As this skit shows, even the person beginning the fight may have a misperception that leads him to be unaware that his partner actually agrees with him. That's why, as we're about to see, it can be extraordinarily helpful to uncover the *real* reasons for our fights.

WHAT DO YOU SEE?

Let's have some fun. *What Do You See?* on your smartphone or tablet presents a few illusions for you to figure out. You can do this with your partner to discover who sees what first. Learn how powerful your differing perceptions are as you both decipher the illusions. In the process you'll see how your perceptions of a particular issue can be dramatically different.

THE REAL REASON FOR YOUR FIGHTS

Because of differing perceptions, the most passionate fights between couples are rarely about the actual content of the quarrel. They are typically about something else entirely.

But what is the "something else"?

Keith Sanford of Baylor University has a pretty good idea. His groundbreaking study, published in the journal *Psychological Assessment,* included 3,539 married couples with ages ranging from eighteen to eighty-five and with marriages ranging from one year to sixty-one years. Sanford analyzed variables such as the words couples chose to describe a past fight and the self-reported feelings and behaviors while each were in the throes of fighting.[3]

What did he find? Every argument, covering everything from dirty clothes on the floor to the meaning of life, resolves itself into two fundamental complaints: (1) one person feels that he or she is being unjustly blamed or controlled because of something that has nothing to do with the argument and (2) one partner feels neglected, and this manifests itself in that partner thinking *You don't really care about me* or *You are not as invested in this marriage as I am.*

> Our life is what our thoughts make it.
> MARCUS AURELIUS

In other words, research reveals that most fights are driven by two fundamental and distinct concerns: perceived threat and perceived neglect. Let's take a look at each.

Perceived Threat

Tim and Sarah, a loving couple, were hanging a heavy mirror above the dresser in their bedroom. Trying to get it positioned just right, Tim told Sarah to move it up a few inches so he could mark the place to put the nail.

"I can't move it any further," she said, feeling pressured. "I'll drop it."

"Just step on the nightstand there," Tim said with a fair degree of urgency.

"It's got your books all over it."

"There's still plenty of room to put your foot on it," Tim continued. "This thing is getting heavy."

That's when it happened. Without warning, Sarah shouted, "I hate your books!" With one swift kick, she sent a stack of them flying.

Tim was baffled. *Did she really just do that? Sarah is a loving woman. Why would she snap at me? Why would she say she hates my books?*

The fact is, Sarah wasn't really mad about the books. But she didn't know that. Rightly or wrongly, she subconsciously perceived Tim to be critical and controlling, maybe even a little judgmental. Somewhere beneath the surface, this thought was working on her emotions: *He has no idea how exhausted I am right now, and he's bossing me around as if I'm a hired hand.*

But this thought didn't register on Sarah's conscious mind. She just knew that she felt pressured and attacked at the moment, and that feeling caused her emotions to erupt all over the handiest target. So, not being aware of her inner perceptions, Sarah focused on a surface issue.

She said, "Your books are cluttering up our bedroom! Do you really need twenty books by your bed every night?"

"Honey," Tim replied, "I have six books there. That's all. Not twenty."

The conversation intensified. They bickered over his books and argued over the mirror for several minutes. Why? For only one _real_ reason: Sarah felt threatened. She may have focused on the clutter, but the true reason for her upset had nothing to do with books. The underlying issue stemmed from the way Tim was aggressively

> Reject your sense of injury and the injury itself disappears.
> MARCUS AURELIUS

directing her and disapproving of the way she was performing a task—or rather Sarah _perceived_ Tim to be directing her and disapproving. That's what sparked the fight.

Whenever someone perceives his or her partner to be aggressive, demanding, overly controlling, critical, or too quick to lay blame, it signals a threat. Whether or not the threat is real, our perception triggers a part of our brain known as the limbic system to prepare to flee or fight. We become defensive to protect ourselves ("I can't read your mind"), or we counter the perceived attack with one of our own to balance the scales ("You're the problem, not me"). Either way, if we don't recognize the real issue (that we feel threatened), we tend to focus on surface issues that may never get resolved.

You feel THREATENED when you perceive your partner as being

- Critical
- Judgmental
- Controlling
- Demanding
- Attacking

Perceived Neglect

David has worked hard at his job all week, and he assumes Saturday is his day to watch a game on television or play a round of golf. Who can blame him? His wife Britney, however, justifiably assumes David should take the kids off her hands for a few hours because she's been wiping runny noses and changing diapers all week. She deserves a break too and expects him to give it to her. Again, it's a pretty reasonable assumption. When these unique perspectives collide at about eight o'clock on Saturday morning, the sparks start to fly.

In this case, neither David nor Britney really feel threatened, but they both perceive neglect. "If David was contributing to this relationship as he should," Britney reasons, "he would do things differently." David is thinking the same thing about Britney. Perceived neglect involves a feeling that your partner is failing to invest in you

> All our knowledge is the offspring of our perceptions.
> LEONARDO DA VINCI

or the relationship. You sense it whenever you feel your partner to be uncaring or uncommitted. In short, you feel neglected.

Perceived neglect occurs when you're hoping for a compliment that doesn't arrive or a concern that isn't shown. It happens when you're ready for affection or intimacy that isn't being reciprocated or when your spouse looks at others in a way you think is inappropriate. Perceived neglect ensues whenever you feel forgotten, unattractive, overlooked, abandoned, helpless, deceived, ignored, or shut out. It can happen over minor matters (she ignored my request for coffee) to major ones (he's flirting with someone online). A person who perceives any form of neglect can sulk and play the victim. Or he can get angry. Or she can point fingers and make accusations. Conflict, of course, results.

As with the perception of threat, we tend to fight about the surface issues when we don't recognize that it's our perceived *feelings of neglect* that are the true cause of our pain. But once we acknowledge the true reason we feel hurt—because we see our partner as failing to make a desired contribution in the relationship or an ideal level of commitment to it—we get to the heart of the matter and dramatically increase our chances for resolution.

> **You feel NEGLECTED when you perceive your partner as being**
> - Uncaring
> - Uncommitted
> - Neglectful
> - Selfish
> - Disengaged

Here's the bottom line. When you identify the perception of either threat or neglect—your own and your partner's—you're getting to the heart of the matter, and you're well on your way to fighting a good fight. Why? Because if you fail to resolve your underlying concerns, you'll fail to resolve the conflict. When most couples argue, they never consider the underlying perceptions. As a result, they focus on less important issues. Does this mean the surface issues are not important? Not necessarily. Most couples have trigger issues or hot topics that seem to generate more heat than they should.

THE REAL REASON WE'RE FIGHTING

Whenever a conflict heats up between the two of you, *The Real Reason We're Fighting* on your smartphone or tablet will help you zero in on the real issue behind your conflict. It will pinpoint the cause as either perceived neglect or perceived threat—or a combination of both. And it's quick. You'll answer just a few questions (taking less than a minute) and receive a bit of pertinent and practical feedback designed just for you. Try it out now, even if you're not currently in a heated exchange. You can use a fight from your past as a model for answering the questions.

THE FLIP SIDE OF PERCEPTION

Johnny Lingo lived in the South Pacific. The islanders all spoke highly of him. But when Johnny went looking for a wife, the people shook their heads in disbelief. In order to obtain a wife in this island's culture, you paid for her by giving cows to her father. Four to six cows were considered a high price for the most beautiful of brides. But the woman Johnny Lingo chose was plain, skinny, and walked with her shoulders hunched and her head down. She was timid and shy. What surprised everyone was Johnny's offer. He gave ten cows for the girl! Everyone believed his father-in-law put one over on him.

Several months after the wedding, a U.S. visitor came to the islands to trade, and he heard the story about Johnny Lingo paying ten cows for a less-than-desirable woman. Upon meeting Johnny and his wife, the visitor was taken aback. This wasn't a shy, plain, and hesitant woman; she was a rare beauty who was utterly poised and confident.

The visitor asked about the transformation, and Johnny's response was simple. "I wanted a ten-cow woman, and when I paid that for her and treated her in that fashion, she began to believe that she was a ten-cow woman. She discovered she was worth more than any other woman in the islands. What matters most is what a woman thinks about herself."

Johnny Lingo understood the power of perception—not from the negative perspective as we've explored it in this chapter, but from the positive side. You see, perception works both ways, and we cannot end this chapter without also noting the power of *positive* perception. Just as our negative assumptions of our partner's motives, attitudes, and actions shape our sense of reality, our positive assumptions do the same.

When we choose to perceive the best motives and put the best interpretation on our mate's actions, we will find that our perception begins to form not merely our sense of reality that may or may not be true, but it can have the effect of re-forming reality itself when our mate responds to our expressed perception of him or her.

Now that we have explored the pitfalls and pluses of perception, we want to give you a revolutionary new tool that we guarantee will help you to increase your odds of having good fights instead of bad ones. That's what is coming up in the next chapter.

HOT TOPICS

The sooner you identify your hot topics, the sooner you'll be able to cool off when one of them flares up. In this applet you'll simply rate how each of the fifteen most common hot topics relates to you. Once your partner has done the same, we'll help you make sense of your combined list, especially when it comes to the topics that top it.

FOR REFLECTION

- What do you think about the power of perception when it causes two people to have differing perspectives? Think of an example of differing perceptions from your own relationship. How did the two perceptions contribute to conflict?

- Do you agree that the real reason underlying almost every conflict in marriage is the perception of threat or the perception of neglect? Why or why not?

- How often do your perceptions define objective reality? Are you able to adjust your perception to see the truth more objectively after hearing your mate's perception? Are you willing to take the steps to try harder to get inside your mate's head in order to resolve conflicts more satisfactorily?

★ CHAPTER 4 ★
WHAT IS YOUR CONFLICT QUOTIENT?

*Never let the problem to be solved become
more important than the person to be loved.*

BARBARA JOHNSON

WE'VE BEEN EAGER TO get to this chapter. As we promised at the end of the previous chapter, we can help you dramatically increase your odds for improving your good-fight-to-bad-fight ratio, and now we're about to show you how. The key is in discovering and understanding what we call your Conflict Quotient, which will prove to be an invaluable guide that will do much to ease tension and promote resolution to your conflicts.

First, let's talk about how to find your Conflict Quotient. Think about an issue that's causing tension in your relationship these days. It may be big or little. It may be new or ongoing. Got one in mind? Now ask yourself these two questions:

- How *important* is this issue to me?
- How *ready* do I feel to work on it right now?

That's it. Once you've answered these two simple questions, you have a sense of your Conflict Quotient. It's easy. The importance of the issue divided by your readiness to work on it gives you your CQ:

$$\frac{\text{IMPORTANCE OF THE ISSUE}}{\text{READINESS TO WORK IT OUT}} = \text{CONFLICT QUOTIENT}$$

Don't worry, your CQ doesn't require any math. It merely requires a moment of reflection to answer those two easy questions. Individually they don't have a right or wrong answer. But the answer the two questions reveal together sheds an amazing amount of light on whatever issue is causing one or both of you trouble.

Your CQ is all about raising your level of awareness. It gives you instant insight on whether your issue is likely to turn into a good fight or a bad one. With a handy app on your mobile device, not only can we give you your CQ, but we can also provide personal coaching on your specific situation. But first we want you to understand how it works. As the two questions imply, it all comes down to two items: importance and readiness. Let's take a look at each of these components.

HOW IMPORTANT IS THE ISSUE?

Couples fight about anything and everything. Sometimes the issue is trivial (putting the cap back on the toothpaste), sometimes important (discussing monetary investments before making them).

We counseled a couple that was fighting about whether the chances of a coin toss were truly 50/50. They'd been arguing their respective sides for a couple of days, and neither recognized how insanely silly the argument was. We know another couple who had a fight about what day of the week a specific date fell on the previous year. But the fight that took the cake was the woman who did not like the way her husband breathed. No kidding! Couples can sometimes fight about the silliest issues.

Of course, other fights are about issues that are critically important. We might have conflict over how we balance our budget—or how we don't. It might be about whether to have a child or how we discipline the child we have. We might fight about feeling disrespected, slighted, or even betrayed. These are not insignificant issues. They deserve serious attention and eventual resolution.

In the heat of battle, however, it can seem that every topic is vitally important. So we have worked out a way to help you determine more objectively the level of importance you place on any issue that comes up. The following chart provides a scale you can use to consider where on the four continuums your own responses might fall for any particular topic of contention:

GRAVITY OF OUTCOME
Will the result of this fight really matter?

Trivial ⟵————————————⟶ Critical

LEVEL OF HURT/SADNESS
Do I feel wounded or down because of it?

Not Hurt/Sad ⟵————————————⟶ Very Hurt/Sad

IMPACT ON VALUES
Is this issue a threat to my convictions or principles?

Nonthreatening ⟵————————————⟶ Conflicts

PREOCCUPATION
How much am I thinking or worrying about it?

Not Thinking About It ⟵————————————⟶ Obsessing About It

The more weight you put on the right end of any of these four questions, the more important this issue is to you.

HOW READY ARE YOU?

"Let's get ready to rumble!" For the full effect, you need to read that sentence in a long, drawn-out voice. Michael Buffer, a professional ring announcer for boxing and professional wrestling, made this his catch-phrase in the early 1980s. Because his style of rolling certain letters and adding inflection is utterly unique, he actually acquired a trademark for the phrase. He even used a variation of it for a Kraft cheese com-mercial: "Let's get ready to *crumble!*"

The difference between being ready to rumble (or crumble) is not a bad distinction for our purposes. Sometimes when faced with a topic that generates conflict, we are more ready to crumble than rumble. In fact, a bad fight always leads to crumbling. A good rumble, however, is another story. The question is, how do you know whether a conflict will be a good rumble? It's partly a question of importance, as we just saw in the four-point continuum above, but equally important is readiness.

Readiness can be tricky. When a verbal skirmish hijacks our conversation and we're about to get embroiled in conflict, we don't typically stop and ask ourselves if we're ready for it. It just happens—ready or not.

But what would happen if, in that moment, you could quickly know whether or not you were ready to rumble? What if you could immediately determine whether the fight would be good or bad? Truth be told, you can. If you are emotionally amped up, if you are

> Only in the world of mathematics do two negatives multiply into a positive.
> **ABBY MOREL**

irritable and hungry, or if you are PMS-ing, you're bound to have a bad fight. The odds are stacked against you. On top of that, some of us who may have a more aggressive personality may even trick ourselves into believing we're ready for a fight when we're not. That's a fatal fighting error (and we'll delve into that in chapter 5).

Here's our simple checklist for determining whether or not you're ready. If you experience any of the following conditions during the conflictual moment, you're not ready to fight:

- I'm hungry or in pain.
- I'm tired or exhausted.
- I'm emotionally charged.
- I'm pressed for time or need to think.

It only takes one of these conditions to spoil a good fight.

YOUR BATTLE ZONES

Once you determine an issue's importance and your readiness to get into it, you'll know your CQ. Matching your readiness or unreadiness against the issue's triviality or importance will enable you to decide whether to rumble. The following chart helps you to do this by cross-referencing the options to create four battle zones. Each zone has its own uniqueness, but only one zone reveals that the issue is worth fighting for.

	TRIVIAL	IMPORTANT
NOT READY	**THE DUMB FIGHT** Not only are you fighting over something that doesn't matter from your perspective, you're not in a good place to fight. This will not end well.	**THE DUMBER FIGHT** You've landed on a topic that matters to you, but you are in no condition to fight. You're at high risk for serious friction and disastrous results if you pursue this fight.
READY	**THE NONFIGHT** You're in a good place to tackle a tough topic, but this topic isn't tough. You see it as trivial. Since your emotions are in check and you're in a good place, this is not a fight for you. It's a conversation.	**THE GOOD FIGHT** This is a fight worth having. It's important and you are ready. When you're in this zone, your odds for fighting a good fight are significantly higher and the end result is much more likely to be positive.

Keep in mind that you are only assessing your CQ, not your spouse's. Your CQ is unique to each of you and to every specific conflict that comes up. This means the battle zone you find yourself in may not match that of your partner. In fact, it probably won't. That difference is often one of the elements that causes the fight in the first place. That's okay. We're going to give you a tool to help you instantly gain fast-acting insight into whatever predicament you're facing.

THE GAME CHANGER: COMBINING YOUR CONFLICT QUOTIENTS

Let's say your partner has a routine of leaving dirty towels on the bathroom floor after a shower. Just because you see that habit as impor-tant enough to be addressed doesn't mean your spouse does. The fact that it's impor-tant to one person and not the other is the reason it creates tension. Not only that, one spouse usu-ally can't understand why the trivial issue is driving the other nuts, while the other can't understand why anyone wouldn't see it as impor-tant. The result is dissonance if not disagreement.

> Being heard is so close to being loved that for the average person, they are almost indistinguishable.
> DAVID AUGSBURGER

But even if a couple is in agreement about a topic's importance, it doesn't ensure that they are aligned when it comes to their readiness to deal with it. One might be ready for a good fight, but if the other is feeling tired, hungry, or pressed for time, for example, you're automatically out of sync on the readiness scale. Anytime one of you is not ready, your rumble is more likely to crumble.

When a hot topic emerges, what would happen if you and your partner were instantly able to combine your two CQs? Well, we can tell you: it's a game changer. When you combine your CQs, you are far more likely to steer clear of bad fights that pull you apart. You're far more likely to have good fights that draw you together.

We could go on to explain the dozens of combinations and the simple steps you can take within each CQ that will enable you to exchange bad fights for good, but it would have little meaning to you until you're in a fight. So let's forgo the detailed explanation and let an app show you how it works.

YOUR CONFLICT QUOTIENT

Your Conflict Quotient on your smartphone or tablet is one of the most important tools we will suggest to you. Why? Because in a matter of seconds, it will not only reveal your personal CQ on a topic, but it will also coach in that moment when you most need coaching to take specific steps based on your personal predicament (the combination of your two CQs together). Each time a conflict heats up, this app will guide you and your partner with personalized information. It will guard both of you from being confrontational, defensive, belittling, and self-righteous. It will help you get to the **CORE** of a good fight (Cooperation, Ownership, Respect, and Empathy). In short, this app will ensure you're fighting a good fight.

IMPULSE CONTROL: THE KEY TO CURBING A BAD FIGHT

So far in this chapter we've shown you how to uncover your conflict quotient in order to increase your odds of having good fights. But there's another private place where bad fights breed, and we'd be remiss if we didn't shine some light on it before closing this chapter. That place is deep down in your brain.

The human brain, as you know, interprets events and stores them in memory. As we saw in the previous chapter, the brain is more of an abstract painter than a realist. Instead of storing information and experiences with absolute accuracy, it more often stores impressions and leaves the interpretation open to thoughts and feelings. We can be thankful, however, that the brain holds something deeper than just thoughts and feelings. It houses a survival drive within what is called the limbic system. This drive is primal and powerful. The limbic system is command central for managing every perceived threat, fear, or hazard.[1] It contains the hypothalamus (which manages biological needs), the thalamus (central to attention and alertness), the hippocampus (where our emotional memories reside), and the amygdala.

The almond-sized structure of the amygdala lies deep in the brain and regulates our major emotions, such as anxiety, depression, affection, and aggression. When the amygdala gives the go-ahead, a blaring alarm is set off in our brain to notify our entire body. The body responds immediately to the alarm. Our lungs take in more oxygen, breathing becomes rapid, our heart rate and blood pressure increase, and our muscles are primed for action. The amygdala goes even further. It tells the hippocampus to draw up from memory any deep-seated wounds in order to add emotional intensity to our body's readiness for defense. Then it sends signals to the front of our brain to inhibit concentration and rational thought, which would get in the way of unimpeded action. In short, the amygdala, if not managed, holds the capacity to hijack our ability to fight well against someone we love.[2] The amygdala is often the culprit for a bad fight, because it turns the rumble into a no-holds-barred, knock-down, drag-out melee.

If you've ever seen someone fly off the handle for no apparent reason, you've witnessed an amygdala hijack. If you've been in a conflict where you suddenly felt overwhelmed by angry emotions, you've experienced an amygdala hijack.

So how do we manage the amygdala? How do we keep it from setting us up for senseless conflict and irrational clashes? The answer is found in our mind. Our mind is what helps our brain to be more objective. It has the capacity to serve as an unbiased reporter on the scene. It can impose on the conflict a more realistic and nonjudgmental perspective. It's not as likely to jump to conclusions. "The mind is its own place," said English poet John Milton, "and in itself can make a

> It's not easy, but if you accept your misfortune and handle it right, your perceived failure can become a catalyst for profound reinvention.
> CONAN O'BRIEN

Heaven of Hell, a Hell of Heaven."[3] Our mind holds the promise of calming the radical impulses of our amygdala. It can cool a hot head and warm a cold heart. For this reason, your mind is the key to curbing bad fights.[4]

At a marriage conference in Washington D.C., a man came up to us during a break. "I've got something to tell you," he said. He went on to describe how he and his wife had been battling over small messes in their home. "I'm very neat, and my wife doesn't even notice when things are in chaos. We've had some real blowout fights over this." He went on to say that he had found a way to deal with the problem simply by reframing it, which completely cured him of picking a fight with his wife over the issue of untidiness.

"What did you do?" we asked.

"This may sound strange," he replied, "but I simply imagined that my wife had died, and then I asked myself, 'If I could bring her back to life knowing I would have to forever deal with messes all over the house, would I want her back?' That's it. That simple exercise gave me a brand-new perspective." The man went on to tell us that this self-made mind game had saved him from countless squabbles with his wife. How? By getting his mind to reframe his point of view.

Your mind holds your sense of self. It is synonymous with your thoughts. Thus you "make up your mind," you "change your mind," and you are sometimes "of two minds." In fact, experts say that the mind is what your brain does. Your mind, in a word, thinks. It helps your brain to be rational.

"The eye sees only what the mind is prepared to comprehend," said philosopher Henri Bergson. This tells us that while the mind is capable of managing the amygdala with objectivity, that's not going to just happen automatically. Your mind will think in the way you train it to think. In other words, if you're looking for worst-case scenarios or unscrupulous motives or bad behavior in your spouse, that's exactly what you'll find. Your mind will make sure of it, because you have trained it to see only what you are looking for. If, on the other hand, you set your mind to see positive possibilities, you're likely to see those instead. That

> Married life teaches one invaluable lesson: to think of things far enough ahead not to say them.
> JEFFERSON MACHAMER

is what the apostle Paul means when he urges us to "be transformed by the renewing of your mind."[5]

So when your spouse asks if you ate the last scoop of ice cream or if you bought something new for your wardrobe, your mind doesn't have to assume negative motives. If your amygdala jumps up and urges you to jump with it and respond with a defensive reply, you can train your mind to remain neutral. It can curb the panic of the amygdala and put judgment in abeyance until you gather more information. This allows you to stave off the often-unreliable perceptions of threat and neglect and dramatically lower your quotient for bad fights.

Your mind makes all the difference when it comes to fighting a good fight.

FOR REFLECTION

- Think of a time when your conflict quotients differed. Maybe the subject of the conflict was not important to you, but it was of vital importance to your mate. How did you resolve the issue? Is it resolved yet? Could you resolve it now that you understand more about how to engage successfully?

- Think back to some of your fights with your mate. How often did the issue really matter to you? How often did you engage in the conflict just to win or to prove you were right? Will the analytic helps in this chapter enable you to prevent that kind of fight in the future? Why or why not?

- At the heart of curbing conflict is our capacity to manage our angry impulses. Do you agree that this capacity is found when we use our mind to set aside snap judgments of our partner's thoughts, feelings, or actions? What's an example from your own life?

★ CHAPTER 5 ★

THE RULES OF FIGHT CLUB

Never go to bed mad. Stay up and fight.
PHYLLIS DILLER

NORM EVANS WAS THE offensive right tackle on the NFL's winningest team ever, the 17–0 Miami Dolphins in 1972. Norm's Super Bowl ring sports a Dolphin figure, seventeen diamonds (one for each victory), his name, and the words "Perfect Season."

If you ask Norm and his wife, Bobbe, about their marriage, however, they'll tell you it's not perfect. Like everyone else, they have had their share of skirmishes. It all started when the two Texas teenagers ran off to elope in Mexico. Nobody thought they'd make it as a married couple. After fifty wedding anniversaries, they are a bit surprised themselves.

Recently this couple came to our marriage class at Seattle Pacific University, and we saw how they have been fighting together for their marriage. For fifteen years or so they've accepted our annual invitation to speak about their relationship to two hundred students in our marriage class at the university. On their last visit, they asked the class for help.

"Our couch is terribly uncomfortable," Bobbe told the students. "So I want to buy a new one. Norm doesn't."

"We bought this couch seven years ago," said Norm. "It's just getting broken in."

"As you can see, we need help," Bobbe confessed. She went on to explain that they were going to work out this disagreement right there in the auditorium in front of everybody. It wasn't scripted or planned.

"So here's the deal," Norm said. "We want you to help us follow some rules, and if we break any of them, we want you to buzz us with the buzzers you'll find under your seat."

Of course, there were no buzzers, so Norm explained: "You'll just need to buzz orally in unison." He had the two hundred students hold out their invisible buzzers and practice a couple of times. They immediately got the hang of it.

"One of our rules is to have an open body posture," Norm said as he arranged two chairs on the platform. "We need to face each other and not cross our arms or legs."

"We also need to stay clear of blaming each other or trying to show why the other person is wrong. If we do that, what are you going to do?" The students, now fully on board, buzzed loudly.

Norm and Bobbe outlined a few more rules. They had to lean in while they were talking. They needed to repeat back, in their own words, what they heard the other person saying before they made a new point. They needed to stay on topic. They had to maintain eye contact (no looking at a cell phone).

"Okay," Norm said, "let's do this."

The couple sat facing each other, both leaning forward, and Bobbe said, "You know how I feel about this couch, and I don't understand why you aren't with me."

"Because it's not a great use of our money right now," said Norm as he leaned back in his chair.

"Buzz!" The students didn't waste any time in pointing out that Norm had violated a rule. He smiled in agreement and leaned forward.

"You feel frustrated because I don't agree that we should buy a new couch?"

"Exactly. I'm very frustrated."

"Can I make a point?" Norm asked.

Bobbe agreed, and Norm explained that it was her choice to buy their present couch, and they couldn't afford a new one every few years.

"You were there when we bought it," Bobbe said. "And by the way, you just bought a new car."

"Buzz!" The students pointed out the infraction on Bobbe's side. In accusing Norm about his car purchase, she had violated two rules: not blaming and not staying on subject.

This exercise went on for a few minutes with Norm and Bobbe deliberately breaking the rules to make their point: a good fight has good rules.

RULES AND TOOLS

Every competition of merit has rules and regulations. Whether it's an NFL game or NBA game, there are rules to follow. The same is true for a friendly game of golf, table tennis, hopscotch, or checkers. Even the Ultimate Fighting Championship with their no-holds-barred melees and tagline "There are no rules!" does, indeed, have rules. Rules are needed to ensure fairness and to prevent injury.

> The tone of our truth-telling can build a wall or a bridge.
> ED WALTZ

Marriage is neither a competition nor a game, but because it sometimes involves conflict, a few good rules will go far toward ensuring a good outcome. This chapter is chock-full of proven strategies for keeping your fights not only fair but also productive, ending with the two of you stronger and closer than ever.

These rules will help you get to the CORE of a good fight. Remember that acronym from our first chapter? The four critical elements essential to keeping your fight healthy and positive are Cooperation, Ownership, Respect, and Empathy. To help you put each of these elements into practice more effectively, we've organized the rules and tools of fight under these four categories. Adopting these rules qualifies you as a full-fledged member of Fight Club.

> The best way to have the last word is to apologize.
>
> JOYCE MEYER

RULES FOR CULTIVATING COOPERATION

Good fighters fight for a win-win. They don't try to prove their point or show their superiority. They have a collaborative attitude that says, "If you win, I win too." We have three proven rules and tools designed to bring more teamwork and cooperation into your disagreements: sharing withholds, rating the depth of your disagreement, and agreeing to disagree when necessary.

Cooperation Rule 1: Share Withholds

In every marriage, spouses hold on to information the other doesn't know about. We call these unshared bits of information "withholds." We have withholds not because we're secretive but because we're traveling at the speed of life. For example, an issue registers in our mind, but just before we get a chance to talk about it, the phone rings or a child needs help.

The issue could be positive or negative. On the positive side, you might be ready to compliment your spouse on the way he or she handled a parenting issue when you suddenly realize it wouldn't be appropriate to say it in front of your child. You plan to tell your spouse later, but time moves along, the thought recedes, and your partner never hears the compliment. That's a positive withhold.

A negative withhold happens when your spouse does something that rubs you the wrong way, but for whatever reason, you aren't able to express your feelings. Maybe it's a joke with a zinger aimed at you. You are in a group of friends and don't want to make your reaction public. Maybe you're just too tired to bring it up in the moment because you know it will involve some tension. So it becomes a negative withhold.

What happens to the negative feelings we bury? They have a high rate of resurrection. They pop up or even explode when we least expect them. That's why sharing withholds is such a valuable rule and tool for cultivating cooperation.

One good way to air withholds is to share them routinely on a weekly basis, an exercise that will take you only ten minutes or so. We can almost guarantee that if you do this each week, you'll see the level of tension in your relationship drop dramatically. You'll avoid all kinds of needless conflict, and you'll also notice an uptick in positive connections.

Here's how it works. Each of you writes two things your partner has done in the last forty-eight hours that you sincerely appreciated but did not acknowledge. For example, you might say, "I appreciated the compliment you gave me on my driving yesterday," or "I appreciated your help in planning my meeting this morning."

Next, write one thing your partner has done in the last forty-eight hours that irritated you. You might say, for example, "I didn't like it when you borrowed my umbrella without telling me," or "I didn't like it when you said nothing about the meal I prepared for us last night."

After both of you have written your statements, take turns sharing them. He shares his three statements, and then she shares hers—or vice versa. Here is an important rule in sharing withholds. The person on the receiving end can only say "thank you" after each statement—even the negative one. That's all. Just "thank you." This rule allows couples to share things that bug them without fearing a blowup or a defensive reaction. It also allows couples to receive critiques in the context of affirmation.

One more thing: once each of you has shared your three withholds, discussing the negative ones is off-limits for thirty minutes. This ensures that you move from reacting to responding. It allows you to gain a bit of objectivity.

Sharing withholds can save you hundreds of hours of needless bickering by diffusing buried emotions. It creates a cooperative spirit within your relationship and keeps you up-to-date with each other's concerns and affirmations. When you do this exercise with the assistance of our app, you're sure to retrain your brain toward cultivating more cooperation.

SHARING WITHHOLDS

We often tell newlyweds to choose their ruts carefully because they're going to be in them for a l-o-n-g time. *Sharing Withholds* helps you bring a new groove into your relationship (by sharing your withholds regularly), no matter how long you've been together.

One of the greatest challenges to sharing withholds is doing it on a routine basis so one of you doesn't have to initiate it. That's where this applet comes in. You simply agree on a time when each of you would like to be reminded to share withholds, say Saturdays at 9 a.m., and this applet gently prompts you. The two of you don't even need to be together to make this work. Trust us. You're going to love *Sharing Withholds* on your smartphone or tablet and what it does for your relationship.

Cooperation Rule 2: Rate the Depth of Your Disagreement

Over the years at our live events for couples, we've given out tens of thousands of little plastic cards, each the size of a credit card.

We call it the Conflict Card, and it's designed to help people rate the depth of their disagreement. It contains a scale from one ("It's no big deal to me") to ten ("Over my dead body!").

> Honest disagreement is often a good sign of progress.
> MAHATMA GANDHI

Rating the importance of an issue enables you to know whether it is worth fighting for. When your partner rates it, you'll have a better idea as to how important it is to him or her—a key element in cultivating cooperation.

Sometimes we can get pretty worked up about an issue when, on reflection, we realize it really doesn't matter. When James and Karen were setting up their first apartment, Karen wanted to paint the kitchen walls light blue. She brought home some paint samples to show her new husband.

"I found the perfect color," Karen said enthusiastically, holding paint chips up to the wall.

"I'm not really crazy about it," Jim said.

"Oh, you'll like it once you see it on the wall. It'll be great."

"I don't know . . ."

The phone rang, and that was the last they talked about it. Three days later, James couldn't believe his eyes when he came home to a light blue kitchen.

"What's this?" he exclaimed. "I thought we agreed not to paint it this color!"

"You said you didn't care, so I went ahead."

"I never said that!"

For the rest of the evening, James and Karen argued—he over feeling betrayed and she over feeling unappreciated. The scuffle could have been prevented if each had known just how important (or unimportant) the kitchen color was to the other. As it turned out, James felt strongly opposed to the light blue, but he didn't express his feeling well. Karen, on the other hand, was eager to set up house. She could easily have accepted another color. Their feelings and how they expressed them were almost polar opposites.

Research shows that the more we understand how important a contentious issue is to us, the more we understand ourselves.[1] To "know thyself," as Socrates said, has been called the high peak of knowledge. Self-understanding enables us to make wise choices. It helps us align ourselves with the lives we want to live. It has the potential to help us dial down the intensity of a conflict and to be more cooperative.

THE CONFLICT CARD

The Conflict Card on your smartphone or tablet is an electronic version of the card you just read about. If you have your smartphone or tablet nearby the next time a disagreement emerges, you'll be able to know quickly not only how deeply you feel about the issue but also how deeply your spouse feels about it. This applet will instantly help both of you move to the same page, enabling you to find compromise and work out a win-win solution.

Cooperation Rule 3: Agree to Disagree When Necessary

Have you ever argued points of logic and conviction until you're blue in the face, yet the two of you just keep going around in circles? No progress is made. No opinions are swayed. That's a sign that it may be time to raise the mutual white flag of surrender and agree to disagree.

Research shows that many problematic issues for couples don't get solved; they get managed.[2] This gridlock is especially true when character differences keep emerging as perpetual problems. Bruce, for example, values organization and neatness. He invests time in getting everything in its place, not just at his desk or in his car, but all around the home. His wife, Teresa, on the other hand, couldn't care less about organization. Her closet is a mess. She invests her time in friends and family more than in squaring away the pantry or a bookshelf. Bruce and Teresa have had countless squabbles over these opposite traits with each trying to change the other. But, of course, that's pointless, because they're up against inherent tendencies. Each of them may inch a bit to the other's side, but in the long run, this is not an argument to be solved; it's a personality difference to be managed. When facing such a difference, the couple's skills should be applied not to solving the problem but to managing it. They need to agree to disagree.

> Committing to stay calm is the first key to committing to staying married.
> HAL RUNKEL

One of the most poignant lines in singer/songwriter Susan Ashton's song "Agree to Disagree" sums it up: "We can have our differences, but that won't change the way I feel about you."

RULES FOR CULTIVATING OWNERSHIP

Good fighters own their proverbial piece of the conflict pie. They know that criticism is for cowards and blame and shame never lead to positive outcomes. Instead, they take the courageous step of admitting a mistake. They know it's not *who* is wrong but *what* is wrong that counts. Here are two rules and tools for cultivating this kind of ownership: (1) apologize when you mean it and (2) practice the XYZ formula.

Ownership Rule 1: Apologize When You Mean It

After denying he'd bet on baseball games while manager of the Cincinnati Reds—an infraction that produced a lifetime ban from the sport in 1989—Pete Rose finally confessed his wrongdoing. He hasn't stopped confessing since. In 2006, Rose began using his website to apologize personally to each fan he had failed or offended. How? By sending them an autographed baseball that reads "I'm sorry I bet on baseball." The price? Just $299 plus shipping and handling.

> If you have learned how to disagree without being disagreeable, then you have discovered the secret of getting along.
> **BERNARD MELTZER**

Not much of an apology, is it? When a confession comes with a price tag, the contrition gets sucked right out of it. That's exactly what gets sucked out of an apology to our mate when we apologize prematurely, halfheartedly, or without real regret. Saying "I'm sorry" isn't enough. Your heart must be in it. The word *apology* literally means "an account or story." That means a genuine apology entails a story of your wrongdoing and regret. It's not a flippant expression of sorrow.

That's why a genuine apology is a profound demonstration of responsibility. Few actions cultivate ownership more than a heartfelt apology.

When was the last time you knew you needed to offer an apology but didn't? One of the most constant decisions you should ever make is to apologize when you are wrong. Why? Because saying "I'm sorry" has the power to repair harm, mend relationships, soothe wounds, and heal broken hearts. It has the power to disarm your spouse of anger and prevent further misunderstandings. It also diminishes regret. While an apology cannot undo past actions, it can, if done sincerely and effectively, undo the negative effects of those actions.

On the surface, apologizing seems relatively easy. It simply involves saying those two little words, "I'm sorry." But we don't always do it when we know we should. Something within our psyche makes it tougher than it needs to be. That something is pride. We'd rather harbor the hurt, it seems, than own up to our negative actions.

Here are a few tips on how to say "I'm sorry." A good apology involves three Rs:

- **Responsibility: "I know I hurt your feelings."**
- **Regret: "I feel terrible that I hurt you."**
- **Remedy: "I won't do it again."**

Unless your apology contains all three of these elements, your spouse will sense that something is missing and will likely feel shortchanged.

Apology experts suggest that you keep your apologies brief.[3] When you apologize over and over again, it seems disingenuous. Finally, steer clear of excuses. When you try to explain your mistake, it sounds like self-justification, which detracts from your remorse and contrition.

SAYING "I'M SORRY"

Almost anyone can apologize by saying "Sorry." A true apology—one that really makes a difference—involves the three Rs. But how do you ensure that your apology includes them? How do you apologize so that it's felt in the heart? *Saying "I'm Sorry"* will show you how. Once you try it, you won't want to apologize without it.

Ownership Rule 2: Practice the XYZ Formula

Snark. Do you know the word? It's a combination of "snide" and "remark." Do you ever make snarky comments in your marriage? It's an easy temptation. We humans are prone to criticism, and when we're upset, irritated, or frustrated with our partner, we generally let it be known. "Do you have to have the TV up so loud?" "You've got to turn off the lights if you're not in the room." "You never seem to pay the bills on time." Critical comments such as these often ignite a fight.

Researchers call it a harsh startup.[4] Studies show that 96 percent of the time, the way a discussion starts predicts the way it's going to end.[5] When it starts with a snarky comment, it's going to end badly.

Every conflict begins with criticism. "You always make us late," or "You never pick up your clothes." You may be thinking, *Well, if some foible is really getting under my skin, what am I supposed to do?* It's a good question, and the answer may surprise you: complain about it. That's right. Research shows that it's actually good for couples to complain about what's bothering them. But before you unroll a long list of complaints to your spouse, make sure you know this: criticism and complaining are miles apart.

> I like a man that grins
> when he fights.
> **WINSTON CHURCHILL**

Critical comments almost always begin with "you," as in "you always . . ." or "you never . . ." Complaining, on the other hand, almost always begins with "I," as in "I feel frustrated when . . ." or "I feel sad when . . ." It may seem like a subtle, semantic change, but to the person on the receiving end, the difference between a criticism and a complaint is like the difference between night and day.

Criticism: "You're so selfish. Do you ever think of my needs when it comes to making love?"

Complaint: "I feel so disappointed when I think we're going to make love and you say you're too tired."

Do you see the difference? A complaint focuses on a specific behavior, while a criticism attacks the other's character. It's cynical and snarky.

When you state a concrete, specific complaint, there is a good chance it will lead, not just to a resolution, but also to an improvement. If you want your spouse to hang up his or her coat instead of slinging it over a chair, complain: "I feel like I have to pick up after you when you don't hang up your coat." That will get you much further than saying, "You're such a slob! I'm tired of having to be your personal maid!" A snarky comment like that can't help but spur your spouse to be defensive. And away you go.

So how can you retrain your brain to turn criticisms into complaints, especially when you're seething with frustration? It's easier than you might think. We call it the XYZ formula, and it goes like this:

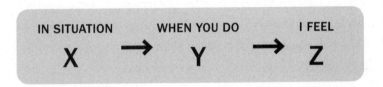

| IN SITUATION | WHEN YOU DO | I FEEL |
| X → | Y → | Z |

That's the formula. You simply fill in the blanks with your particular gripe. "When we are on the road (X), and you change the radio station without asking me (Y), I feel like I don't even matter to you (Z)." That's very different from saying, "Who made you king of the radio?" Or "Last Thursday on our date night (X), when you called your mom and talked for a half hour (Y), I felt hurt because it took away from our special time with each other (Z)." That's far more productive than saying, "You always mess up our date nights." Using the XYZ formula will help you avoid insults and character assassination, allowing you instead to simply state how your partner's behavior affects your feelings. It helps you to own your feelings rather than project your frustrations onto your partner.

THE XYZ FORMULA

If you'd like a little assistance in applying the XYZ formula when you feel the urge to be a little snarky, this tool on your smartphone or tablet is for you. It will help you transform your criticism into a complaint. You can even use this quick and handy applet in the heat of a moment, when you want to be sure you're taking that mental pause to say what you mean and say it right.

RULES FOR CULTIVATING RESPECT

Good fighters steer clear of contempt. Nothing good ever comes from belittling your partner. That's why respect is so essential. This core element creates a sense of safety even in the tumultuous throes of chaos. When two people remain respectful of each other, they recognize differences but maintain honor, civility, and value within the relationship. That's not always easy to do, but the following two rules and tools will help: (1) don't be cruel and (2) take a time-out if needed.

Respect Rule 1: Don't Be Cruel

A married couple had a quarrel that ended with each giving the other the silent treatment. A week into their mute argument, the man had to get up at 5 a.m. to catch a flight to Chicago for a business meeting.

Not wanting to be the first to break the silence, he wrote on a piece of paper, "Please wake me at 5 a.m."

The next morning, the man woke up at 9 a.m., and his flight had long since departed. He was about to confront his wife when he noticed a piece of paper by the bed.

He read, "It's 5 a.m. Wake up."

We may laugh at the absurdity and cruelty of the story, but even kind and caring couples can become painfully disrespectful when their conflicts get serious.

Contempt is the word many researchers use for cruelty. John Gottman identified it as the single most important predictor of a couple's failing relationship. Contempt—that attempt to make your spouse feel about an inch tall—is toxic to love.

> When love and skill work together, expect a masterpiece.
> JOHN RUSKIN

It poisons a good fight. It's sneaky too. If we're not vigilant, it can seep unnoticed into the corners and crevices of our conflicts. Even correcting your partner's grammar during an argument is a sign of contempt. It says, "You're stupid and I'm superior." Rolling your eyes when your spouse is talking is a sign of contempt. It's belittling. So is assuming a patronizing, lecturing tone of voice. Both your verbal and nonverbal actions can communicate contempt.

Contempt is powered by a low but steady dose of adrenaline that propels you to hang the problem on some defect of your partner. "If you weren't so selfish . . . or lazy . . . or irrational . . . or devious . . . we wouldn't be in this mess." Contempt saps your sense of respect for your spouse and fuels your sense of self-righteousness. If criticism is the barrier to ownership, contempt is the barrier to respect.

You may think you're off the hook because you haven't called your partner stupid or lazy or selfish. Don't be so sure. You can accuse your spouse of these defects without ever naming them directly. "I've been with the kids all day, running around like mad to keep this house going, and when you come home from work, you plop down on the sofa and expect me to have dinner ready like I've got nothing else to do." When a wife delivers that sentence in the wrong tone of voice and with the wrong facial expression, she's spewing contempt. Her husband is sure to get the message: he's being accused of being a selfish and inconsiderate person.

The toxicity of contempt is contagious. If your spouse is contemptuous, you're more likely to become contemptuous unless you make a determined effort to remain respectful. If your partner has shot down your character, your natural tendency is to fire up your angry arsenal of contemptuous counterattacks. "Oh, so I'm the stupid one, huh? Everyone knows you're a regular Einstein." Once a couple becomes cruel, the gloves come off and the fight gets ugly.

Gottman says that contempt is not only the most important predictor of divorce, but it can even predict how many colds a spouse will get. He explains, "Having someone you love express contempt toward you is so stressful that it begins to affect the functioning of your immune system."[6]

The surest antidote to contempt and cruelty is appreciation. The more couples look for and acknowledge positive things in their relationship, the more they will like each other. Appreciation builds admiration and fondness. It inoculates against contempt.

Gottman urges couples to build a "culture of appreciation." His studies have found that happy couples develop a habit of mind whereby they scan the environment for things to appreciate about each other. When you create a culture of appreciation in your home, you safeguard your marriage against cruelty.

COUPLES CONCIERGE

Can you imagine having a person work around the clock to assist you in being the best partner you could be? It would be a full-time job, and it would ensure that you didn't forget anniversaries and other important things. Well, *Couples Concierge* won't stand outside your door like a butler, but it's right there on your phone or tablet and is always on call. So why not ask it to help you increase your number of appreciative comments toward your spouse? You'll see a noticeable difference in your relationship within just a couple of days.

Respect Rule 2: Take a Time-Out If Needed

Some years ago we were granted a leave of absence from Seattle Pacific University to be scholars in residence at Oklahoma State University with a special assignment to be the governor's "marriage ambassadors." For twelve months we crisscrossed the state and spoke at Rotary Clubs, universities, and churches. It was an all-out effort to put a spotlight on building strong and lasting marriages.

One night a few months into this endeavor, we were exhausted and hungry. We were sitting in our sparsely furnished rented home when a conflict erupted. Neither of us can remember what it was about—some inane issue involving the dishwasher and a broken plate or something. All we remember is that the conversation got more and more heated until our three-year-old son, John, said, "Daddy, does Mommy need a time-out?"

That's all it took for us to regain some perspective and have a good laugh. In fact, John's line has sometimes been called up to diffuse a heated exchange all these years later. Why? Because on occasion we *do* need a time-out. All couples do.

When either person feels too upset or negative to follow healthy problem-solving steps, it's time to take a break. Experts say that agreeing in advance to take a time-out if one partner

> Marriage is the hardest thing you will ever do. The secret is removing divorce as an option. Anybody who gives themselves that option will get a divorce.
> WILL SMITH

becomes overwhelmed is crucial for avoiding a downward spiral you'll regret later. As Harry Emerson Fosdick said, "No one can get to peace by pouncing on it."

Here are the essentials for having a productive time-out:

- Include in your time-out agreement the understanding that you'll get back to your discussion within twenty-four hours.

- If you're the one ready to blow, stop the conflict by saying, "I need a time-out." Some couples use the T sign coaches employ to signal for a time-out.

- Affirm your intention to solve the problem together later. In other words, don't just leave. Say something like, "I want to resolve this, but I can't do it right now. I'll let you know when I'm ready."

- Stop the discussion immediately and go somewhere to calm down. It takes at least twenty minutes for the body to slow itself down after being worked up.

- Take a walk, read a book, cook a meal, or take a bath. Don't spend your time ruminating about the conversation or having bad thoughts about your spouse.

- Tell your spouse (even with a text or an email) when you will be ready to reengage. Say something like, "I'll be ready to continue in one hour," or "I'll be ready before dinner tonight." Giving a deadline for the time-out to end is essential.

- If possible, before you talk again, try first to share an everyday activity together to reestablish a close, calm connection.

It is impossible to have a rational discussion in a climate of hostility and disrespect. Taking a time-out is one of the easiest ways to rekindle respect for your spouse and keep a fight from escalating. So when you're overheating, don't be afraid to cool off, calm down, and gain some perspective.

TIME-OUT

One of the most important aspects of a good time-out between couples is being clear about when you are ready to reengage the discussion. If you've used *Your Conflict Quotient* on your smartphone from chapter 4, you've already seen how this works. If you haven't, check out the CQ applet and take advantage of the time-out portion.

RULES FOR CULTIVATING EMPATHY

Good fighters step into each other's shoes. Trading places is the quickest way to ensure a positive and healthy outcome from conflict. Nine times out of ten, research shows, our squabbles can be resolved if we do little more than accurately see the problematic issue from our partner's perspective. This is a challenge, of course. Empathy is hard work. These two rules and tools, however, make it much easier: (1) read your partner's mind and (2) send up a prayer.

Empathy Rule 1: Read Your Partner's Mind

Believe it or not, everyone is a mind reader, especially in marriage. In any interaction, we comprehend the meaning of the words we hear spoken, we monitor facial expressions and body language, and we register the speaker's cadence and tone of voice. Why? To get inside our partner's mind. Researchers at UCLA call this perceptual

> Love is seeking to act for the other person's highest good.
> JERRY COOK

ability "mindsight." We use mindsight in the most heated argument and in the most lighthearted chat. We constantly collect clues as to what's on our partner's mind.

But truth be told, we're not very good at it. We often misread our partner's intentions or misinterpret their feelings in ways that are miles from the truth. Although we may deploy as many as three thousand different expressions each day, the vast majority of us are terrible at detecting the feelings they convey.

At a deeper level, we may sense what's going on in our partner's mind by catching what they are feeling. Emotions are, in a sense, contagious. Studies show that in conversation we often unconsciously mimic other people's behavior, speech, rhythms, gestures, expressions, and physical attitudes. This bit of inadvertent aping helps us to gain a direct sense of the other's feelings and psychological attitudes.

All this effort, often unconscious, helps us to size up what our spouse is feeling. After a little interaction, a husband might come to believe that Jane must be on edge about her job. He may be right. But the tension he senses also might be a figment of his imagination, because our life experiences color our mindsight. Our history, biases, and memory distortions can make us read ulterior motives into straight-forward statements, causing us to project feelings onto our partner that don't exist.

> We loved with a love that was more than love.
> EDGAR ALLAN POE

Decades of research on mind reading—or, as psychologists call it, empathic accuracy—reveals that the thoughts and feelings of others, including those closest to us, are far from transparent. In one significant experiment, strangers were videotaped as they conversed with each other. Afterward they reported their second-by-second thoughts and feelings as the conversation progressed as well as their assessments of their counterpart's thoughts and feelings. The results showed that they read each other with an average accuracy rate of 20 percent. Close friends and married couples nudge that up to 35 percent. "Almost no one ever scores higher than 60 percent," reported psychologist William Ickes, the father of empathic accuracy.[7]

Still, we keep trying to read our partner's mind. But should we? Some say we should not because it leads to trouble. But in our opinion, trying to stop couples from reading each other's minds is like trying to stop cats from chasing mice. Since we're going to try to read our mate's minds anyway, we encourage couples to be deliberate. We've been doing this for years, and we've taught it to countless couples. Don't worry, you won't have to sit on the floor swami style and wear a funny turban. Here's how it works.

When either of you runs the risk of making an assumption or reading something into a message, simply say, "I'd like to read your mind." When your partner agrees, explain what you perceive and ask for verification by saying, "How accurate am I?"

Next, your partner rates how accurate (or inaccurate) you are on a one-to-ten scale—ten being right on the money and one being at the far end of the galaxy. Here's an example.

She: "I'd like to read your mind."

He: "Be my guest."

She: "Last night at dinner when you made that joke about the number of minutes I used on my cell phone, you were thinking that I spend too much time talking to my sister. Am I right?"

He: "That's about a three. The thought went through my head, but not for long. I was really wondering if we should get a new phone plan."

Or consider a couple who is thinking about a major move across the country because of a new job offer.

He: "I'd like to read your mind."

She: "Okay."

He: "I think that even though you say you are willing to move our family to Philadelphia, you really want to

stay put. I think you're afraid of disappointing me or
holding back my career. Am I right?"
She: "Yes. That's about an eight or nine. I'm afraid to
speak up on this because I know you are excited about
this opportunity."

You get the idea. This little exercise cuts through all the smoke and
mirrors of potentially misinterpreted messages. It allows you to put your
fears and frustrations on the table to see if they're valid. What's most
important, it helps you to put yourself in your partner's shoes and better
understand her or his perspective. Beware: this tool falls flat if you're not
operating from a base of genuinely wanting to understand your partner.

I WANT TO READ YOUR MIND

You're doing it on the sly already, so why not make
reading your partner's mind more explicit? That way
you'll get immediate feedback on how accurate you
are and avoid any half-baked misperceptions. *I Want
to Read Your Mind* makes it easy. Both you and your
partner will love how quickly it will help you empathize.
Use this tool on your smartphone or tablet often and
you'll be more in tune more often and more accurately
with each other.

Empathy Rule 2: Send Up a Prayer

William Nicholson's stage play and movie *Shadowlands* portrays the
relationship between world-renowned writer C. S. Lewis and American
writer Joy Gresham. Their growing friendship led to a marriage of
convenience. The Oxford professor wed the single mother in a secret
civil ceremony so Joy could gain English citizenship. Eventually it was
discovered that Joy had terminal cancer, and in the process of dealing
with her illness, Lewis realized his love for her.

Joy's cancer went into temporary remission, and for a season she and Lewis experienced the depth of committed love. During this time, an Anglican priest talked with Lewis about prayer.

"I know how hard you've been praying," the priest said, "and now God is answering your prayer."

"That's not why I pray, Harry," Lewis responded. "I pray because I can't help myself. I pray because I'm helpless. I pray because the need flows out of me all the time, waking and sleeping. It doesn't change God, it changes me."

Maybe you've already discovered the abiding power of prayer in your marriage. If so, you know how prayer can change you.[8] It lowers your defenses and opens your eyes to your partner's perspective. It joins your sprits, even when your differing temperaments, ideas, and tastes threaten to divide you.

By the way, for all those skeptics who think prayer is for uptight people who can barely mention the word *sex* without blushing, researchers have found something surprising: couples that pray together have better sex lives. Furthermore, a study at the University of Texas, San Antonio, published in the *Journal of Marriage and Family* showed that 83 percent of couples who pray together describe their relationship as very happy, compared to 69 percent of those who don't pray together.[9] Praying couples are also healthier. After interviewing

> Find the good—and praise it.
> ALEX HALEY

more than a thousand people about the nature of their prayers, Neal Krause at the University of Michigan found that praying for your spouse reduces stress and strain in the person doing the praying, making empathy far easier.[10]

Frank Fincham, eminent scholar and director of the Florida State University Family Institute, researched the impact of prayer on marriage. "We recruited people to participate in a four-week study where they

> You can't shake hands with
> a clenched fist.
> INDIRA GANDHI

were randomly assigned to either pray for their partner, engage in general prayer, or set aside time to think about the positive things in life and about their partner," he said. "Twice a week they were asked to record online what they had done."

Fincham's research showed that spouses who prayed for their partner showed a greater willingness to forgive the other for a transgression. Other surveys of couples married twenty-five years or longer found that forgiveness was one of the most important characteristics of their enduring relationship, allowing them to stay happily married even when coping with conflict. "Our research shows that praying for your partner can bring you back to the common goals," said Fincham. "When people pray, they become one with their spouse. A subtle shift occurs. Praying regulates your emotion, and it never leads to anger."

I PRAYED FOR YOU

Praying for your partner is easy for some and challenging for others. *I Prayed for You* on your smartphone or tablet improves the experience no matter where you fall on that continuum. It gives you a variety of options for improving your prayer life as it relates to your relationship. It makes it easy and convenient to let your mate know how you're praying for him or her.

THE POWER OF A GOOD RULE

For years the mobs of people fighting to catch a cab at New York's busy Penn Station led to appalling episodes of conflict and even violence.

Harried people did terrible things just to get in front of someone else who was hailing a cab.

The Taxi and Limousine Commission solved the problem very simply. They painted a yellow stripe down the sidewalk and labeled it "Cab Line." That's all. It utterly transformed people's behavior. Now, everyone, almost all the time, simply waits in line with no need of any police to enforce order. All that was needed to restore civility was a good rule to follow.

It's difficult to question the value of a good rule that works. In this chapter we've given you nine workable CORE rules to manage your couple conflicts. Let's sum them up:

For more Cooperation . . .
- **Share withholds**
- **Rate the depth of your disagreement**
- **Agree to disagree when necessary**

For more Ownership . . .
- **Apologize when you mean it**
- **Practice the XYZ formula**

For more Respect . . .
- **Don't be cruel**
- **Take a time-out if needed**

For more Empathy . . .
- **Read your partner's mind**
- **Send up prayers for your partner**

You're bound to find some of these rules and tools more helpful than others, because every couple has different tendencies that need to be addressed. What matters is that you use what works for the two of you. As you implement the rules for your own fight club, we're confident you'll get to the CORE of a good fight.

FOR REFLECTION

- One of the rules encourages you to take a time-out when needed. Have you ever done that when a conflict was getting too intense? What happened? Can you think of an exchange where you would have benefited from taking a time-out but didn't? The result?

- Of all the rules noted in this chapter, which one do you think will be most challenging for you to follow and why?

- In reviewing the nine rules in this chapter, which ones are you most likely to implement in your fight club and why?

★ CHAPTER 6 ★

UNCOVERING YOUR PERSONAL FIGHT TYPE

*When all think alike,
no one thinks very much.*
WALTER LIPPMANN

"WOW! YOU MUST NEED a lot of help with your personality," my friend Kevin said while standing in front of a bookcase in my study. "I stopped counting after twenty-five." He was referring to the number of personality textbooks that line a couple of shelves. "How could there be that much to say about people's personalities?"

It's a good question. Every year new books are published on the subject, not to mention thousands of articles in professional journals and the pop psychology in supermarket tabloids. Every autumn semester for many years running, I (Les) have taught a university class titled Personality—a course you'll find in every undergraduate psychology curriculum in every college in the country.

We humans, or at least we psychologists, never tire of trying to understand what makes people tick. Cracking the code of our emotions, attitudes, motivations, and behavior—what we collectively call personality—can be traced back at least to an ancient Greek physician, Hippocrates. He proposed four categories of personality types, or temperaments, and we've been categorizing personalities ever since. In fact, there are hundreds of reputable and respected theories of personalities. No wonder we have so many books on the subject.

We all want to know why people do what they do, and social science has come up with some pretty helpful explanations. More than 80 percent of all Fortune 500 companies test the personalities of their employees to facilitate team building.[1] Some offices literally have their employees' personality profiles posted outside their cubicles on the premise that knowing how someone is hardwired makes it easier to get along with him or her. That's also true in marriage.

Some time ago we worked with a team of professionals to develop a sophisticated online tool that helps couples understand the dynamics resulting from the combination of their unique personalities. It's called the L.O.V.E. Style Assessment. Every day we hear from couples who find tremendous value in discovering how their personality profiles shape their relationship.*

We've all got a personality. It's influenced by our background and our biology, and it holds the key to explaining everything from how we approach affection to how we raise children. More to the present point, personality has plenty to say about how we handle conflict. In fact, understanding how your personality hard-wiring impacts your approach to conflict is essential to preventing bad outcomes in couple fights.

We have a name for the way your personality influences your approach to conflict. We call it your Fight Type. We dedicate this chapter to helping you uncover your own Fight Type, because couples who understand their respective Fight Types are far more likely to fight a good fight.

---

* The L.O.V.E. Style Assessment takes ten minutes and provides you with approximately fifteen pages of personalized information. It reveals much more than how you handle conflict. It also reveals how your personality approaches sex, money, communication, and more. If you're interested, go to LesandLeslie.com and use the word LOVE to receive a discount.

LOVE IS A BATTLEFIELD

When Tim Keller moved his family to New York City to start Redeemer Presbyterian Church, he asked his wife, Kathy, to grant him three years of long hours. After that, he promised, things would change.

Kathy agreed to Tim's request. But when the three-year mark came and went, Tim said, "Just a couple more months." Several more months flew by with no change. Although Kathy reminded Tim several times to honor his promise, she was incredibly patient and restrained about his continuing long work hours. She was, however, determined to get Tim's attention and effect a change. Tim writes what happened next:

> An individual's self-concept is the core of his personality. It affects every aspect of human behavior.
> JOYCE BROTHERS

So one day, Tim came home to a startling smashing noise coming from the balcony: first one smash, then two. Stepping outside to investigate, he found Kathy on the balcony floor with a hammer and a stack of their wedding china, two broken saucers at her feet.

Tim was shocked, but Kathy calmly said, "You don't realize that if you keep working these hours you are going to destroy this family. . . . This is what you are doing." And she smashed a third saucer.

Kathy was able to explain her arguments forcefully, but with emotional control; and when she saw that he was truly listening, they hugged. Afterward, Tim said, "I thought you were having an emotional meltdown." Kathy smiled, "The cups [to those saucers] have been broken for years. I had three saucers to spare. I'm glad you sat down before I had to break any more."[2]

What does this pivotal interaction reveal about Tim and Kathy's personalities? For one thing, it shows that Kathy is a patient woman.

She didn't nag him for three years. She signed up for the agreement, and only when the time was right did she carefully stage her confrontation. That takes discipline. Only a certain kind of personality does that. The story also shows something about Tim. He is a hard-driving man who keeps his eye on the goal—

> You can tell a lot about a person by the way he/she handles these three things: a rainy day, lost luggage and tangled Christmas tree lights.
>
> MAYA ANGELOU

unless something dramatic happens to shift his attention. When it does, he flexes to make it right. Again, not every personality does that.

Numerous characteristics are at play in everyone's personality, but this snapshot of Tim and Kathy highlights two characteristics that are critical to everyone's Fight Type: (1) expressiveness and (2) flexibility. These two dimensions define your approach to interpersonal tension. Expressiveness reveals how willing you are to talk about what's troubling you. Flexibility reveals how willing you are to accommodate what's troubling your partner. How these two characteristics combine determines your Fight Type.

EXPRESSIVENESS: DO YOU TALK ABOUT WHAT'S TROUBLING YOU?

A man from Berlin, Germany, took an unusual approach in trying to bring peace to his marriage. CNN reported that he used an old air-raid siren to stun his wife into submission.

"My wife never lets me get a word in edgeways," the man told the police. "So I crank up the siren and let it rip for a few minutes. It works every time. Afterward, it's real quiet again."

Police confiscated the 220-volt rooftop siren after neighbors filed complaints. His wife of thirty-two years said, "My husband is a stubborn mule, so I have to get loud."[3]

You might say this couple has issues. One of them is clearly their extremely differing levels of expressiveness. You don't have to go to such extremes, however, to see how expressiveness plays out in a typical marriage. It's not unusual for some people to be more expressive about their preferences than others. They become animated when they talk. They speak louder and longer than others. If something is troubling them, they are likely to let you know.

On the other hand, inexpressive people are slow to show emotion and can be difficult to read. They're not inclined to talk it out—at least until they gather their thoughts. If they're troubled by something, you may not know it. They may keep it inside until they've carefully thought through what they want to say.

Of course, few people fit neatly into one camp. Expressiveness is a continuum, as we see in the two columns below. Which side do you identify with most?

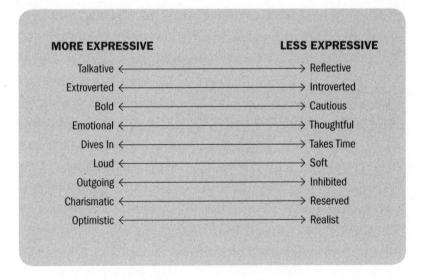

MORE EXPRESSIVE		LESS EXPRESSIVE
Talkative	←————————————→	Reflective
Extroverted	←————————————→	Introverted
Bold	←————————————→	Cautious
Emotional	←————————————→	Thoughtful
Dives In	←————————————→	Takes Time
Loud	←————————————→	Soft
Outgoing	←————————————→	Inhibited
Charismatic	←————————————→	Reserved
Optimistic	←————————————→	Realist

Expressiveness is simply an indicator of how willing you are to talk about what's troubling you. Of course, the more inclined you are to complain, the more likely you are to have conflicts.

FLEXIBILITY: DO YOU ACCOMMODATE WHAT'S TROUBLING YOUR SPOUSE?

Imagine that you've just picked up your car after a routine tune-up. The service technician says, "This car is in great shape. It runs perfectly, and I didn't have to do a thing to it." Later that day, your brakes don't work. You discover that your brake fluid was dangerously low. You could have been killed.

You go back to the shop and say, "Why didn't you tell me?"

The technician replies, "Well, I didn't want you to feel bad. And, to be honest, I was afraid you might get upset with me, and I want you to like me."

Such a response would make you furious!

The same thing happens when spouses avoid speaking the truth to one another because they don't want to lose their partner's approval. They gloss over troubles in an attempt to maintain peace. They forget to mention the overdue bills. They walk on eggshells to avoid causing conflict. They try desperately to not make waves. They're eager to please and willing to flex with their partner's whims and desires. It is in their nature to do all they can to keep things on an even keel and to soothe relational rifts.

> In the course of my observation, the disputing, contradicting and confuting people are generally unfortunate in their affairs. They get victory sometimes, but they never get good will, which would be of more use to them.
> BENJAMIN FRANKLIN

Other spouses tend toward the opposite. A little conflict doesn't bother them. They're not about to walk on eggshells in order to accommodate anyone's feelings. They're more inclined to say what's on their mind. They dig in their heels and stand their ground. Some call them stubborn or determined because they're often unyielding about their perspective. In short, they're not afraid of a little dustup.

Flexibility, like expressiveness, is a continuum. Consider the two columns of trait descriptions below. Does one side describe you more than the other?

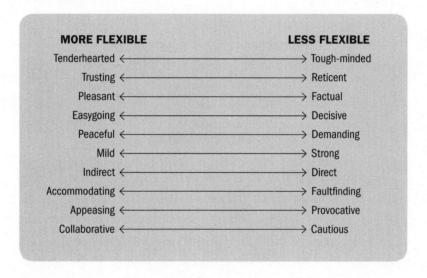

MORE FLEXIBLE	LESS FLEXIBLE
Tenderhearted	Tough-minded
Trusting	Reticent
Pleasant	Factual
Easygoing	Decisive
Peaceful	Demanding
Mild	Strong
Indirect	Direct
Accommodating	Faultfinding
Appeasing	Provocative
Collaborative	Cautious

Flexibility is a measure of how willing you are to accommodate your spouse's troubles. The more inclined you are to flex, the less likely you are to cultivate conflict.

THE FOUR FIGHT TYPES

Once you determine how expressive you are of your own desires and how flexible you are in meeting the desires of your spouse, you'll find that you fall into one of the following four quadrants:

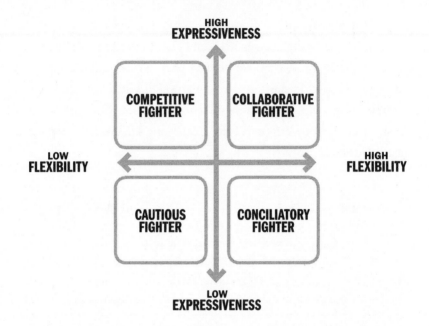

As you can see, you are a Competitive Fighter if you are highly expressive and less flexible. You are a Collaborative Fighter if you are highly expressive and highly flexible. And so on. Of course, you may be at home in more than just one of these quadrants. You may be a combination of a Cautious and a Competitive Fighter, for example.

WHAT'S YOUR FIGHT TYPE?

Now that you've read about fight types, take the online *Fight Type Inventory* to get a personal read on your personal approach to conflict. When both of you take this assessment, it's guaranteed to be an eye-opener. You'll receive our feedback (via video) on your two unique combinations of Fight Types. When you begin discussing your results, you'll quickly see how valuable your new insights will be in helping you both fight a good fight. You don't want to miss this fun self-test.

EXPLORING YOUR PERSONAL FIGHT TYPE

In this section we will describe the personality characteristics that make up each of the four Fight Types. If you are not yet sure of your own Fight Type, the following descriptions will help you to determine it. If you already know your own Fight Type, you may prefer to zero in on that section only. While you will certainly find value in reading about each of the four types, we've designed this section so you can skip the descriptions that don't apply and go directly to the one in which you're interested.

The Competitive Fighter

You like to win. You tend to be more expressive about your troubles and less flexible in accommodating your partner's viewpoints. You are goal-oriented and aggressive. You're often direct and to the point, and your desire to win means you can come off as blunt or even tactless. When you're duking it out, your tongue can have a sharp point to it, whether you mean it to or not. You may also be an impatient listener, especially when stressed. In other words, you probably figure out what your spouse is trying to say long before he or she has finished saying it, and you're eager to jump in and throw a counterpunch even while the other is talking.

> The difficulty with marriage is that we fall in love with a personality but must live with a character.
> PETER DEVRIES

When your spouse disagrees with you, it only fortifies your determination to win. "My wife will take a stand and stick to it no matter what," a newly married husband told us. "She becomes so convinced she's right that she doesn't spend any energy trying to see my side. I feel like I'm married to a prosecuting attorney." That's life with you if you're a Competitive Fighter. It's not that you don't want to find a solution, you just want—ideally—for your spouse first to acknowledge that you are right.

In fact, you probably don't like to let conflict linger. You want to get it out on the table and find a resolution. Of course, that's not always easy in a relationship that requires compromise. As a person who doesn't struggle with being indecisive, humility may be one of your biggest hurdles in fighting a good fight. As a Competitive Fighter, you can often benefit from working on the C in the **CORE** of a good fight—*cooperating* to fight for a win-win.

The Collaborative Fighter

You are a team player. You tend to be expressive and flexible. You listen well and love being listened to. The more your spouse listens, the more you feel loved. You're also adept at moving the conversation away from the central issue in order to be as accommodating as possible, especially if it helps to sidestep a tough topic.

You are inclined to steer clear of conflict. You may avoid directly confronting the issue at hand, even if your spouse wants to discuss it. You will sometimes bury your own needs or conceal your own desires simply to avoid tension. At times you might even swallow your feelings and wear a smile to conceal your distress. When things get rough and you're feeling especially stressed, you might withdraw from the relationship altogether and resort to sulking.

> There is little difference in people, but that little difference makes a big difference.
> **W. CLEMENT STONE**

Be aware that conflict avoidance is different than conflict prevention. The former is unhealthy and the latter is not. Chances are that you do both. In addition to avoiding conflict by concealing your true feelings, you also prevent potential conflict in your marriage by knowing and avoiding what is likely to trigger a heated disagreement with your spouse. As a Collaborative Fighter, you can often benefit from working on the E in the CORE of a good fight—*empathizing* with your spouse to be sure you accurately understand what he or she thinks and feels.

The Conciliatory Fighter

As a person who is less expressive and highly flexible, you strive to be a peacemaker. As a result, you're typically on the quiet side, keeping many of your feelings carefully hidden from view. You probably don't divulge details unless you're asked about them. You approach your conversations with a sense of serenity and calm, and your spouse needs to draw you out patiently. Even if the point of controversy is urgent or exciting, you express it evenly and without heightened emotions. You tend to speak slowly and deliberately.

Since peace is just about your highest priority in marriage, you don't experience many external quarrels with your spouse. You keep your conflicts covered up, internalizing your struggles. You rarely, if ever, have an emotional outburst of any kind, and certainly not one of anger. Other Fight Types may air their grievances and stir up tension, but not you. Conflict, for you, is to be avoided at all costs. That may mean burying any unpleasantness that is sure to bring about dissension. It may mean avoiding a particular topic that is bound to cause turmoil. Whatever it takes is fine with you—as long as it maintains the peace. As a Conciliatory Fighter you may find it especially beneficial to work on the O in the CORE of a good fight—*owning* your piece of the conflict pie.

The Cautious Fighter

You are thoughtful and guarded. You are less expressive but also less flexible. You like to focus on the facts, but you'll also probe for the hidden meaning behind your mate's words. You'll often ask specific questions of your partner as you seek to understand an issue at a deeper level. You'll sometimes ask the same question again until you find the reassurance, feedback, and reasons for your partner's viewpoint. In almost all your conversations with your spouse, you need information and time to consider carefully whatever is being discussed.

Many of your fights are the result of your feeling criticized or because you have read something into your spouse's motivations. Once the disagreement begins, you tend to be very rigid and overly detailed. That is, you may quote what your partner said—even from conversations you had days or weeks earlier—and cite specific instances to back up your points. Instead of verbalizing your conflict, you may even be apt to write a long note that gives a detailed and logical explanation of your grievance. As a tactic, you may also ask questions, much like an attorney, that push your partner into a corner, proving how you are correct and your partner is wrong. This may cause your spouse to feel belittled.

> I love being married. It's so great to find that one special person you want to annoy for the rest of your life.
> RITA RUDNER

You don't enjoy fighting, but you generally keep your wits about you in the process, unless your failure to convince your spouse causes you to withdraw in a morose and moody way. As a Cautious Fighter, you may find it especially beneficial to work on the **R** in the **CORE** of a good fight—*respecting* your partner to be sure he or she doesn't feel demeaned.

AM I STUCK WITH MY FIGHT TYPE?

Now that you are aware of your personal Fight Type, you may wish you could change it and you wonder whether you can.

The French philosopher Albert Camus said, "We continue to shape our personality all of our life." That's certainly true when it comes to the parts of our personality that influence how we fight. Whether you are competitive, collaborative, conciliatory, or cautious, you can always improve the way your handle conflict.

The basic hard-wiring for your temperament is relatively non-negotiable, but you can choose which aspects of your personality to accentuate or moderate. For example, if, as a Competitive Fighter, you know you tend toward being opinionated and uninhibited, you can learn to control these tendencies when you need to. Or maybe you're a Careful Fighter, and it's in your disposition to be more subdued and matter-of-fact—a tendency that causes you to get chided for never showing your emotions. You can learn to counter this a bit when it might be helpful.

So don't think for a minute that you can blame your dark side on your God-given personality. You can't say, "Well, I yell a lot because that's just the way I am, and I can't do anything about it." Nope. That's not true. Your Fight Type is not a license to be flagrant with the parts of your personality that can make a bad fight worse. Quite the opposite. Now that you're aware of your personal Fight Type, you can do more than ever to ensure that your personal approach to conflict is healthy and productive. In short, becoming aware of your Fight Type becomes a significant asset for fighting a good fight.

FOR REFLECTION

- What personality assessments have you taken? What do you know about your personality as a result? How does this information inform your Fight Type?

- Based on what you've read in this chapter, where would you place yourself in one of the four Fight Type quadrants? What is your personal Fight Type? What personality factors influenced your choice?

- Now that you know your Fight Type, are you content with it? Why or why not? If not, what controls can you place on tendencies that might impair your marital conflicts?

★ CHAPTER 7 ★

LEVERAGING YOUR FIGHT TYPES TOGETHER

A long marriage is two people trying to dance
a duet and two solos at the same time.
ANNE TAYLOR FLEMING

WHILE ATTENDING A MARRIAGE seminar on communication, David and his wife listened to the instructor declare, "It is essential that husbands and wives know the things that are important to each other."

He addressed the man, "Can you describe your wife's favorite flower?"

David leaned over, touched his wife's arm gently, and whispered, "It's Pillsbury all-purpose, isn't it?"

It's a silly little joke, but it makes a point. There is great value in uncovering and understanding your personal Fight Type, as we hope you did in the previous chapter. But there is equal value in understanding your partner's Fight Type as well. We hope the two of you have a good conversation together about your two types. That will help you greatly in reaching a better understanding of each other and the dynamics of your conflicts. To assist you in that direction, we want to pass along some advice—just a few nuggets for improving how you relate to your partner's Fight Type. As in the previous chapter, you can, if you like, skip the sections below that don't pertain to you.

IF YOU'RE MARRIED TO A COMPETITIVE FIGHTER . . . SET SOME BOUNDARIES

"This above all," said Shakespeare, "to thine own self be true."[1] It was his Elizabethan way of saying, "Build some boundaries for yourself." If you're married to a Competitive Fighter, you may find plenty of opportunity to spar, dancing around the ring and debating the same issues over and over—how one drives the car, the way dinner is prepared, and so on. When you identify a boomerang issue that won't go away, call a marital meeting. Build a boundary.

In this meeting, talk about who is best at certain tasks and who should control them. If you are a better cook, you should be in control of the kitchen, and the Competitive Fighter needs to agree to stay clear. If he or she is better behind the wheel, he or she should drive the car. The trick to making this strategy work is to remind the Competitive Fighter of your agreement. If your spouse starts telling you how to cut carrots, for example, say, "We agreed that this is my domain, and I am in control here." Maybe such delegated roles seem too formal and prescribed for you. The truth is, they sometimes *can* be. But negotiating your preassigned roles can help you set healthy boundaries and ease your life with a Competitive Fighter by getting him or her to back off.

You can also build a boundary whenever your spouse attempts to cut you down to size. If he or she is hurling insults, call a time-out. Call a penalty. Say something like, "That comment is out of bounds, and I won't stand for being spoken to like that." The idea is to build a boundary that protects you from being bossed around if your Competitive Fighter starts to be a bully.

IF YOU'RE MARRIED TO A COLLABORATIVE FIGHTER . . .
ASK FOR HONESTY

"Say what you have to say, not what you ought,"[2] said Henry David Thoreau. That's hard advice for a Collaborative Fighter to swallow. It can be extremely frustrating for some spouses who truly want an honest opinion from the Collaborator they married. Why can't they get the honest opinion they are looking for? Because Collaborators don't like to hurt the other's feelings, so they have a tough time delivering conflicting opinions or bad news. Even if they don't like something that's going on in the marriage, they'll often put a positive spin on it to avoid confrontation.

Let's say that as a surprise for his spouse, a husband wallpapers the bathroom on his day off. When she comes home, he proudly shows her what he's done.

"Wow!" she says. "You really worked hard on this."

The husband presses for details. "Yes, but what do you think? Now that it's up, I'm not sure it works."

"It's lovely," his wife affirms, but he suspects she doesn't really like it.

That is often what you may face when married to a Collaborative Fighter. You really want your spouse to weigh in honestly, but all you get are complimentary platitudes. What can you do? Remember, the last thing your spouse wants to do is offend you.

> The goal in marriage is not to think alike, but to think together.
> ROBERT C. DODDS

That's why you'll need to move things forward with a little nudge. Many times, all that's required is a straightforward request for an honest opinion: "I really want to know what you're thinking. I want your honest feedback." An invitation to be honest, to speak one's mind, is what the Collaborative Fighter needs in order to open up with any expression of negativity related to your work. Make it clear that his or her opinion and even criticism won't offend you.

For example, instead of saying, "What do you think about this letter I wrote?" say "If you were me, what would you change about this letter? I really need some honest and objective input." The more you invite direct feedback, the more your spouse is likely to see that being honest with negative information is not as divisive or intimidating as he or she thought.

IF YOU'RE MARRIED TO A CONCILIATORY FIGHTER . . .
DON'T PUSH OR PRESSURE

Have you ever seen your spouse freeze up and become immobile? Let's say you're running errands at a quick clip in order to make it to the restaurant across town where you have dinner reservations. You need to pick up a prescription, but you can't find a parking place at the drugstore. So you urge your spouse to get out of the car and pick up the prescription while you circle the block. "Just jump out and go straight to the counter. I'll circle the block, and to avoid the light going the other way, I'll meet you on the opposite side of the street when I come around."

"What?" your spouse calmly asks.

"Just go," you snap. "I can't stay stopped much longer because there are cars behind me."

But your spouse just sits there in the passenger seat almost in a daze, as if suffering from brain-lock. You wonder what's going on. You speak more sharply. "Are you going to do this or not?"

Well, the reason your Conciliatory Fighter has become immobile is because you've gotten too pushy. If you want your spouse to get moving, you've got to stop shouting. Yelling produces paralysis in Conciliatory Fighters. They don't respond well to pressure. In fact, they tend to shut down in the face of it.

If you want to motivate a Conciliatory Fighter, you need to coax with kindness. Say something like, "Since we can't find a parking space, how do you feel about me letting you off here to pick up the prescription while I circle the block in the car?" Your spouse will quite likely respond positively to this approach. It doesn't sound so urgent, so loud, or so pressure-packed. That makes all the difference. Coaxing with kindness is one of the most practical and effective ways of loving your peace-loving partner.

IF YOU'RE MARRIED TO A CAUTIOUS FIGHTER . . . DO WHAT YOU PROMISE

Your Cautious Fighter spouse can be a perfectionist and somewhat demanding. No doubt you know that already. But it may help to know that these demands often stem from high levels of anxiety that surface when you don't measure up to his or her high standards. Of course, those standards may not be legitimate, but the anxiety your spouse experiences about them is real. Your Cautious Fighter feels extremely apprehensive when you break a promise or fail to meet deadlines or goals. If you say you're going to have the front closet cleaned out before the weekend, and Friday night arrives and it's still not done, your spouse begins to feel that you're not trustworthy. *What other projects are you failing me on?* he or she wonders. And the anxiety climbs.

> When introverts are in conflict with each other . . . it may require a map in order to follow all the silences, nonverbal cues, and passive-aggressive behaviors.
> ADAM S. MCHUGH

The common human tendency is to push back on the seemingly unreasonable expectations a spouse may have about how the lawn should be mowed, when the bills are paid, how the pantry should be organized, and so on. We know it may be difficult, even somewhat humiliating, to live under the implied disapproval of a spouse with overly high expectations. But we suggest that you lay aside your pride for the greater good and do your best to follow through on your projects, big or small, in a way that you know will please your Cautious Fighter.

When you do this, it will not only make your spouse feel more loved, but we believe it will also do much to alleviate the problem. It will also lower your mate's anxiety level about you in general—and that goes a long way in helping to relax his or her unrealistically high standards.

By the way, you can also help your spouse relax his or her standards for perfection by making reassuring reports on your progress. Simply saying something like, "I'm making great progress on that project. It's coming along really well." A comment like that lightens the anxiety load of a Cautious Fighter. It helps him or her to breathe easier and feel more assured and comfortable.

> Words kill, words give life; they're either poison or fruit— you choose.
> PROVERBS 18:21, MSG

But let's make this clear. If you have a pattern of breaking your promises, that's a flaw in your integrity that you need to address regardless of your partner's Fight Type. You can better love your spouse—and it's especially true with a Cautious Fighter—when you not only follow through on what you say but when you follow through at a level that completely fulfills your promise. This will make any spouse happy, and it's a sure way to curb conflict in your home.

COMBINING YOUR FIGHT TYPES

When you look at the possible combinations of Fight Types, ten pairings emerge. We're not going to dwell on them at length, but here's a snapshot of each combination. One of these parings is yours. Reading your particular combination will give you a quick summary of its strengths and challenges.

Competitive Fighter and Competitive Fighter

You are both strong-willed and neither of you hesitates to put on the gloves, get in the ring, and duke it out. The good news is that you both speak your mind, so you don't need to guess what's troubling the relationship. The challenge, of course, is to cooperate and work toward a win-win outcome. That's not easy for two competitors.

Collaborative Fighter and Collaborative Fighter

This is, in some respects, the least combative combination of Fight Types. Both of you are inclined to voice your troubles, but you do it in a tactful way. That keeps conflict from getting stirred up. Of course, this doesn't mean you are without your moments of tension. But when they arise, you tend to be respectful and work together toward a mutually satisfying solution.

Conciliatory Fighter and Conciliatory Fighter

On the surface, your marriage may seem to be conflict-free. You are both dedicated to keeping the peace. Neither wants to stir up trouble, so you keep mum about what's troubling you. As a result, you often walk on eggshells, making for some uncomfortable moments that sidestep issues that really need to be addressed.

Cautious Fighter and Cautious Fighter

The two of you are not likely to fight frequently, and when you do, you move slowly into sparring. Both of you calculate your moves. You give serious thought about what you want to say. As a result, your fights may last longer than most. When things get really rough, the two of you are also at risk of icing each other out by giving the other the cold shoulder.

Competitive Fighter and Collaborative Fighter

If you're the competitive one in this relationship, you need to count your blessings for a flexible spouse who is willing to get in the ring with you and work things out. It's likely that the longer you're married, the better you've become at managing your sparring matches equitably. They may get intense, but they typically don't last long.

Competitive Fighter and Conciliatory Fighter

The two of you may have a great marriage, but when you start to duke it out, it's an unfair match. The Conciliatory Fighter will throw the fight every time. This may irritate the Competitive Fighter on occasion, but it makes for a pretty peaceful relationship most of the time—as long as the Competitive Fighter has learned to pull punches and the Conciliatory Fighter is not dealing with bottled-up unhappiness.

Competitive Fighter and Cautious Fighter

If this is your Fight Type combination, the two of you have one thing in common: you both fight for what you want, but you fight for it in different ways. The Competitive Fighter is vocal and spontaneous. The Cautious Fighter is quieter and calculating. The very difference in your styles can exacerbate your conflicts. That's why the two of you must take care to ensure that you show each other respect.

Collaborative Fighter and Conciliatory Fighter

You two are almost too focused on meeting each other's needs to have too many knock-down-drag-outs. Each of you is flexible and eager to find resolution without having too much tension enter the relationship. But since the Collaborator is more inclined to voice troubles, the Conciliatory Fighter—eager to keep peace—may place his or her needs in abeyance. Over time, this can lead to resentment.

Collaborative Fighter and Cautious Fighter

With this combination, your fights are pretty low-key compared to other couples. You may have your share of tension, but you rarely raise your voices. Instead, you both put the issue on the table. It may not reach the table immediately, because the Cautious Fighter needs time to think before being ready to talk about it accurately. When you do put it on the table, you talk it through rationally.

Conciliatory Fighter and Cautious Fighter

Both of you are dedicated to keeping the peace. That's good. You rarely, if ever, have loud shouting matches. Instead, you both work to keep the problem from becoming bigger. This is a good thing as long as your conciliatory and cautious natures don't cause you to withdraw. This can actually be a dangerous combination, because it increases the possibility of that kind of withdrawal. When one partner tries to relate with the other and the other partner withdraws, it is seen as a lack of interest, and that's damaging. Overall, the Conciliatory-Cautious combination has some positive advantages as long as you both observe this caution.

> Loyalty means giving me your honest opinion, whether you think I'll like it or not.
> COLIN POWELL

IT'S NOW UP TO YOU

One school of thought in psychology says, "Awareness is curative." In other words, simply becoming aware of an issue is often enough to help you improve it. We hope this chapter has heightened your awareness of how your Fight Type and that of your spouse interact to handle conflict. That's why it's important for you to identify and understand not only your own Fight Type but also that of your partner. Both Fight Types are involved in every conflict, and your ability to work toward a successful outcome depends on knowing how your two Fight Types work together. Our prayer for you is that you and your spouse will use this knowledge to work toward making every fight a good fight. We've done our best to give you the tools, and the rest is up to you.

FOR REFLECTION

- How does the information you've learned in this chapter affect the way you and your partner handle conflict?

- Have you and your spouse discussed how your individual Fight Types affect your approach to conflict? If so, what was the result? If not, what can you do to improve the way your Fight Type interacts with that of your partner?

- As you consider how your two Fight Types combine in your relationship, what is the greatest strength you bring to the table? What is your greatest challenge in terms of making your two styles work together effectively?

★ **CHAPTER 8** ★
FIGHTING THROUGH THE BIG FIVE

Marriage means expectations,
and expectations mean conflict.

PAXTON BLAIR

IMAGINE HAVING A REFEREE, wearing a black-and-white striped shirt and a whistle hanging from his lips, preside over your next marital tiff. The official would watch the two of you spar until one of you could be declared the winner. As strange as it sounds, the following real-life couples actually know this experience:

- Reita Robinson wants her husband, Joe, to tame their daughter's hair. Joe thinks their daughter should wear it wild as a form of self-expression.
- Kurt Green thinks his wife, Wendy, is obsessed with sending cards. Wendy likes being nice.
- John D'Annunzio says his wife's accent pillows are ridiculous. Machaeline says they make the house prettier.
- Donna Pulgiano wants her husband, Frank, to stop talking to so many strangers. Frank thinks it's harmless.

Each of these couples and their ongoing arguments were featured on the television show *The Marriage Ref,* which debuted on NBC in 2010.

The show's premise involved real-life couples in-studio to face a panel of experts composed of celebrities and comedians such as Alec Baldwin, Madonna, and Ricky Gervais, who weigh in and decide which spouse is right. Host Tom Papa (the ref) made the final call and declared one of the spouses in each combating couple the winner.

The goal, according to the show's producers, was to give couples something they have always wanted but have never had—a clear winner. Near the end of each episode, the studio audience voted to make one of the winners "the rightest of the right." These winners received twenty-five thousand dollars and their own billboards, displayed in their hometowns, declaring they were right.

Apparently, finding out who's right wasn't as watchable as the network hoped. The show was a big flop, receiving an overwhelmingly negative reception from critics and audiences alike.[1] Why? Perhaps people didn't like the idea of making light of marital disputes. Or maybe it was the idea that celebs with not-so-successful relationship track records are dispensing marital judgments. Or maybe it was the lineup of bickering couples who seemed to have been overly coached, even for a so-called reality show. Or could it be that the idea of labeling one partner right and the other wrong just didn't sit well with the public.

Personally, we think the problem may have been that the fights were mostly tedious. We doubt that audiences related to many of the fight topics. Talking to strangers and accent pillows? Really? Are these the issues couples are fighting about? It's true that many marital squabbles can be about nothing. It takes very little for the fur to fly in most marriages. But the fights that really stir things up, the fights that matter most, are never about greeting cards and hairstyles. There are certain predictable hot topics shared by most couples that ignite the most combustible conflicts.

A lot of couples fight some; some couples fight a lot. But almost all couples fight over the same five things: money, sex, work, parenting, and housework. And most argue about these five issues over and over again. In part, that's because they are hot buttons for almost everyone—stressors that speak to our sense of love and fairness.

Few of us are looking for a marriage ref to point out who

> Never let a problem to be solved become more important than a person to be loved.
> **BARBARA JOHNSON**

is right and who is wrong in these five areas. A fight that ends with a winner and a loser is the antithesis of a good fight. We are, however, looking for ways to minimize conflict. That's exactly what this chapter is about. Not only will we explore why each of these issues is a tinderbox in most marriages, we will also give you some proven tools to help you cool down these hot topics. Let's jump in.

FIGHTING THROUGH MONEY

Scenario 1: After buying a giant new flat screen without discussing the purchase first, your spouse is now yelling at you for spending too much on a pair of shoes.

Scenario 2: You and your spouse are at odds over how much to save for retirement. You want to spend money now and enjoy life. Your spouse wants to save as much as possible.

Scenario 3: Your church announced a major campaign to raise money for drilling wells in Uganda. The pastor is asking every member to give beyond what they normally give. Sounds good to you. But it doesn't sound so good to your spouse.

Most couples face numerous issues like these on a regular basis, and any one of them can ignite a financial conflict. According to an AICPA survey in the *Wall Street Journal*, numerous studies report that couples fight more about finances than any other issue. The survey revealed the following stats:

- On average, couples fight about money at least three times per month. That made it the most volatile topic, ahead of fights about children, chores, work, or friends.
- As couples age, they generally argue about money more often.
- The most common cause for money arguments (58 percent) focused on differing opinions of needs versus wants.
- Forty-nine percent of couples argue about unexpected expenses, and 32 percent argue about insufficient savings.
- Thirty percent of married adults have engaged in at least one deceitful behavior related to their finances (such as hiding purchases).
- Despite all the conflict about money, 55 percent of couples said they do not set aside time on a regular basis to talk about financial issues.[2]

Another study of 2,800 couples by the National Survey of Families and Households found financial disputes to be a strong predictor of a couple's stability.[3] Even more eye-opening, those couples who report disagreeing about money matters once a week are over 30 percent more likely to divorce than couples who report financial disagreements a few times a month.[4]

If a couple can learn to fight a good fight about finances, they will help their marriage enormously. So what's the secret? You can certainly do the obvious basics: curb excessive spending, agree on a budget, dig yourself out of debt, cut up your credit cards, discuss major purchases, and devise a savings plan. These are wise actions, but we suggest you go deeper.

How to Curtail Your Currency Conflicts

Believe it or not, money fights between couples are rarely about money. The sooner you understand this, the sooner you'll overcome them. Money represents power, security, values, and dreams. Nearly any financial conflict you have can be traced back to a fear related to one of these important issues.

In Scenario 1, the fight between the spouse who bought a flat screen and the one who bought an expensive pair of shoes was not really about how much either had spent. It was over who had power and how the other might threaten that power. Whenever one person controls the purse strings, it's a power play. That spouse is in charge of more than just

> Money doesn't talk, it swears obscenity.
> BOB DYLAN

money. He or she is treating the other like a child, and conflict is inevitable.

In Scenario 2, the couple at odds over how much to save for retirement were not really fighting about saving or spending. It was over security. One partner, the saver, carries more anxiety than the other about their future well-being. When the other spends money that could be going toward that security, anxiety increases—as does the likelihood of conflict.

The fight in Scenario 3 was not about money for wells in Uganda. It was over values that represent generosity and other personal spiritual matters. When one spouse resists the other's desire to give toward a cause, there will be conflict.

The point is that financial fights are rarely about money. They are about much deeper and more important matters. It's no wonder that money tops the list as the topic couples fight about most! Look at what it represents: power, security, values, and dreams.

So if you want to minimize a currency conflict, trace it back to the fear that's fueling it. Instead of fighting over the amount of money that was spent on who-knows-what, shift the focus toward what really matters: (1) your fear of not having influence in important issues impacting your life, (2) your fear of not having security in your future, (3) your fear of having no respect shown for your values, or (4) your fear of not realizing your dreams.

By keeping the conversation focused on these deeper issues, you're more likely to stay within the **CORE** of a good fight. Money matters bring out our selfish sides. They cause us to play the blame game and become disrespectful. But when the *real* issue emerges, it has a way of helping both partners Cooperate, take Ownership, show Respect, and practice Empathy. Why? Because the deeper issues entail more vulnerability. And vulnerability begets vulnerability. It keeps the conversation focused on what matters most to both of you.

MONEY TALKS

If you experience more than your fair share of friction over finances, you'll want to be sure you use *Money Talks* on your smartphone or tablet. It will give you additional insights and practical applications, not only for talking through your money, but also for implementing some new practices.

FIGHTING THROUGH SEX

Have you ever had a nagging suspicion that, in bedrooms across the country, on kitchen tables and other places too scintillating to mention, married couples are having more and better sex than the two of you?

You're not alone. It's tough to imagine a culture more conducive to feelings of sexual inadequacy. Sex is everywhere. It's in films, television, music videos, and advertising.

The sexual saturation of our world leads many couples to think there's something wrong with their sex life. Nowadays, sexual dissatisfaction can apparently be monetized.

> Sex is a conversation carried out by other means. If you get on well out of bed, half the problems of bed are solved.
> PETER USTINOV

A recent article in *Time* magazine was titled "French Man Forced to Pay Ex-Wife a Settlement for Lack of Sex."[5] Citing "lack of bedroom activity," the court awarded fourteen thousand dollars to the forty-seven-year-old ex-wife whose needs were apparently not met during the twenty-one-year marriage.

Sex. According to almost every study on the topic, it's in the top tier of issues causing couples consternation and conflict. Why? Because our culture imbues us with an expectation that if we were like other normal couples, we'd be having bed-shaking sex all the time. The issue of frequency, however, is a matter of perception. In the film *Annie Hall*, Woody Allen and Diane Keaton are shown split screen as each talks to an analyst about their sexual relationship. When the analyst asks how often they have sex, he answers, "Hardly ever, maybe three times a week." She answers the same question with, "Constantly, three times a week."

Frequency seems to be the crux of the conflict for married couples. Most are not fighting over kinky stuff. Asked to rank their favorite sex acts, almost everybody (96 percent) found penile-vaginal sex "very or somewhat appealing." Oral sex ranked a distant third, after an activity that many may not have realized was a sex act: "Watching their partner undress."[6]

Frequency is a relatively easy issue to resolve and well worth the effort. According to the Pew Research Center, adults rank a "happy sexual relationship" as the second most important factor in making a marriage work, behind "faithfulness." So let's see what we can do to reduce sexual conflicts and get your libidos in sync.

How to Minimize Your Sex Fights

We know from research that couples' sex lives fall into three groups. One-third have sex twice a week or more, one-third have sex a few times a month, and one-third have sex a few times a year or not at all. If you're in the first group—the one-third who have sex twice a week or more, and especially if you're not newly married—count your blessings and move on to the next section of this chapter. For the rest of you, we have a suggestion.

To keep sexual grievances down and the marital bedsprings bouncing, we recommend focusing on solving "coordination failure." It's a common problem in marriages. The number-one reason people report not having sex in their marriage is "Too tired," followed

> The best position is no substitute for a healthy relationship.
> **KEVIN LEMAN**

closely by "Not in the mood." Most of the time, that's code, knowingly or not, for having mismatched libidos. In other words, the problem of frequency is the result of coordination failure.

In a perfect world, you and your spouse would have flawlessly matched libidos all the time, but we all know that's an unrealistic fantasy. But if you're feeling out of sync, we can help you get better coordinated.

First, you've got to get over the common misperception that your spouse doesn't want sex as much as you do. If that's what you choose to believe, you'll find what you're looking for. One of the best ways to equalize the scales of sexual desire is to put an end to snide comments or innuendos that highlight a perceived libido difference. Every time you say something, even under your breath, like, "Well, if we ever had sex . . ." you're driving a sexual wedge between you and your mate. Set your mind so that you see your spouse as being on the same side with you. This is the C in the **CORE** of a good fight—an attitude of *cooperation*.

Next, discuss your sex drives. As we write this, we can almost feel you cringing. For most couples, talking about sex is about as comfortable as sleeping in a car. Yet it's a conversation that's critically important to aligning your libidos and minimizing your conflicts. When the time is right, when both of you are relaxed and not distracted, ask each other to explain when you feel most frisky. Your answers may surprise you. A friend recently discovered that his wife found him sexiest when he wore a suit. He joked that he was thinking about wearing it to bed. Learn as much as you can about each other's sexual desires. Ask about the time of day, as well as the time of month, when your partner is most inclined to want sex. Ask what would make it easier, more desirable, or more fun.

Make sure that part of this conversation involves how you both initiate sex. In couple's counseling, we often hear that one partner doesn't like to initiate sex. If you're married to someone like this, you've no doubt attributed your partner's shyness to a lack of libido. That's a mistake. Instead, make it easier for him or her to initiate sex. Find a sign or a signal that will make this almost effortless. For example, the interested mate might light a candle or play a particular song or give a certain look that would be their come-on signal. You get the idea. So don't waste time. Talk about what could be used to make the initiations easier.

Before we leave this topic, let me (Les) have a word—make that a paragraph—with our male readers. It's a tidbit of advice I first gave in my book *Crazy Good Sex*. Let's say that to really enjoy sex, you need to be in a particular mood. You need to feel completely safe and understood by your wife, and this needs to begin long before you even think about jumping into bed. To become sexually aroused, you need some warm-up time that might begin with several minutes of gentle caressing interspersed with pillow talk. The lights need to be low, you need to consider what you're wearing, and you need some time to brush your teeth and prepare yourself physically. Hard to imagine, right? But I'm sure you're getting the point. Just in case you're not, I'll spell it out: what I've just described is exactly what most wives need. If you want your wife to be more forthcoming with her sexual desires, you've got to do your part in helping her love your lovemaking sessions. A little *empathy* (the **E** in the **CORE** of a good fight) can go a long way toward getting you to slow it down a bit and set the stage for passionate sex that makes her feel great.

LET'S TALK ABOUT SEX

To eliminate the cringe factor for you in having this conversation, we've designed an applet that makes it much easier. You can use it not only to initiate the conversation in a way that's not as awkward for you but also to help you articulate the more personal aspects of your sex life without turning fifty shades of red.

FIGHTING THROUGH WORK

A strange but telling thing happened as we spoke to a large group of professional couples some years ago. Our topic was "Winning at Work Without Losing at Love." Immediately after our session, the two founders of BlackBerry smartphones were introduced to speak about their company. The response was startling. Amid the applause were audible boos from every corner. Many of the spouses didn't appreciate how the handheld devices, so helpful in business, had stolen their mates away from their marriage.

The imbalance of work and marriage is the catalyst for plenty of conflict between couples. Chances are that one or both of you eats, drinks, and breathes work. You're always talking and thinking about it, even on vacation. Your spouse is far more important than your career, but it doesn't always seem that way to him or her.

Why does work become such an issue? To begin with, more time and energy are spent at work than on any other waking activity. Sixty-eight percent of us spend more than nine hours each day on the job, including commuting time. More than one in five of all employed adults bring work home at least twice a week.

We complain about work. We sometimes try to avoid it. We call in sick to get out of it. But the truth is, we need purposeful

> A career is a wonderful thing, but you can't snuggle up to it at night.
> **MARILYN MONROE**

work—not for the money alone but also for a sense of personal worth. Work provides spiritual, psychological, and emotional fulfillment. Sigmund Freud said that to live well we must learn to love well and to work well. The poet Kahlil Gibran said, "Work is love made visible." For most of us, work, whether paid or unpaid, gives us identity.

Cartoonists and storytellers assume that most people who toil for their daily bread fantasize about winning the lottery. With their winnings clutched in their fist, they can tell the boss what he can do with his old job, kick the Xerox machine, pack up their laptop, and hit the road. But this assumption paints a false picture. In a national survey, more than three-fourths of the respondents said they would choose to remain in their same jobs even though they had, by good fortune, received enough money to live comfortably for the rest of their lives.[7]

You may wonder what these people would really do if they won the lottery. The Institute for Socio-Economic Studies in White Plains, New York, wondered the same thing. They looked up more than a thousand people who had won a million dollars or more in a lottery. Only 16 percent actually retired from work altogether. Four out of ten kept working at the same job they had even though they had no need for the income.

It's only natural to see your husband's obsession with work as a threat to your marriage. But reminding yourself of how strongly his career is linked to his sense of identity and self-worth may help you put this drive in perspective. We have, however, a more practical and proven suggestion to help you balance the marriage-work scale while minimizing your work woes.

How to Curb Your Career Conflicts

We've got two words for you: date night. We know. You've heard this a thousand times: do a weekly date night or your marriage will suffer. Sounds more like a threat than friendly advice, doesn't it? But it's a surefire way to keep career conflict to a minimum.

In spite of this frequent advice, the message doesn't seem to be getting through. Here's how often married people, aged twenty-five to fifty with two or more children, have a date night:

- Once a week: 4 percent
- Once a month: 21 percent
- Once every two to three months: 21 percent
- Once every four to six months: 18 percent
- Once every seven months or less often: 36 percent [8]

Yikes! We can do better than that, and there's good reason to do it. The National Marriage Project at the University of Virginia recently released a report titled "The Date Night Opportunity." This study found that husbands and wives who set aside a deliberate time to connect and have fun at least once a week were approximately three and a half times more likely to report being "very happy" in their marriages. When University of Minnesota researcher David Olson surveyed more than ten thousand married couples, he found that togetherness was a top priority for 97 percent of happy couples but for only 28 percent of unhappy pairs.

The facts are clear: the happiest couples make a habit of having a date night. It resets the imbalanced scales of a marriage that has gotten out of whack with too much work.

How do you go about dating in marriage? First of all, find activities you can both look forward to. If one of you is into sports and the other is interested in art, don't make your date nights a tug-of-war between stadiums and museums. Find a mutual

> The older I get, the less time I want to spend with the part of the human race that didn't marry me.
> ROBERT BRAULT

interest that gets you both excited. Couples who go on dates both enjoy have fewer fights. That's because if you're having a problem, you'll say to yourself, "This is the same person I had a blast with on Saturday night." The lingering glow will provide motivation to work it out.

Even better, do something neither of you has tried before. Remember when the two of you were first dating? *Every* date was exciting. Why? Because everything you did together was new. The entire experience of exploring each other's personalities was exciting. Fast-forward a few years and a different picture emerges. You know each other well, and life has become far more routine—the same restaurants, the same conversations. While familiarity can be comforting, it can also induce a sense of boredom. But what if you were to do something novel on some of your date nights? Would it "bring back that lovin' feeling"?

Researcher Arthur Aron from the State University of New York at Stony Brook put this question to the test.[9] He recruited couples and produced a roll of Velcro tape, explaining that they were about to take part in a game. Couples who got eager and excited were asked to move to another group. To ensure the accuracy of the study's outcome, he wanted participating couples who were not into games. Aron's assistants used the Velcro to secure the couples together—the right wrist and right ankle of one to the left wrist and left ankle of the other.

Resisting the temptation to hum Lionel Richie's "Stuck on You," the researchers covered the floor with pads and placed a large foam obstacle in the middle of the room. They handed each couple a large pillow and instructed them to hold the pillow between them while crawling on their hands and knees to the obstacle, climbing over it, and then crawling back to their starting point. The couples who had been dismissed were asked to do something far more mundane, like roll a ball to a designated spot while their partner watched from the sidelines.

> Occupation is the necessary basis of all enjoyment.
> LEIGH HUNT

The experiment was designed to see if by doing something fun and unusual, they could create feelings similar to when the couple first met and their dates were more exciting. To that end, the couples in both groups completed several questionnaires, rating, for example, the degree to which their partner made them "tingle" and "burst with happiness." As predicted, the couples who conquered the giant foam obstacle were far more loving toward one another than those who had the duller ball-rolling task. The Velcro couples made significantly more positive comments about their partners than the ball rollers.

The point? Don't make your date night the same predictable activity every week. A movie and dinner is great, but shake it up now and then. Also, don't overlook pockets of child-free time at home. Instead of watching television or catching up on email after the kids are in bed, slip out to the deck for a little stargazing. Or enjoy a Saturday morning date while your teenager snoozes until noon. The idea is to capture little dates when you can. They don't always require a baby-sitter or advanced planning. Building a weekly date is the best way to curb career conflicts.

LOVE TALK STARTERS

If too many work issues are pushing the two of you into the boxing ring, you can probably benefit from the sage advice of dating each other again. A date can be big or little. Either way, you want to make sure your conversations during these escapes bring you closer together. *Love Talk Starters* on your smartphone or tablet is designed to do just that. It provides dozens of conversation starters you can access right on your phone. Some are lighthearted. Some are more meaningful. All of them are love talk starters.

FIGHTING THROUGH PARENTING

Once your baby is born, you undertake a huge commitment. Experts estimate that you'll spend 157,250 hours parenting that child.[10] A recent Pew Research survey asked 770 parents why they decided to have kids. Of those surveyed:

- **Seventy-six percent said it was because of the joy of children.**
- **Fifty percent said it was to appease their spouse or partner's wishes.**
- **Forty-seven percent said it was because they had adequate financial resources.**
- **Thirty-five percent said "it just happened".**
- **Fifteen percent said it was because they wanted someone to "care for me when I'm old".**
- **Four percent said it was because of pressure from their family.** [11]

It's good to know that the majority of parents recognize and are motivated by the great joy of having children. But regardless of the reasons for becoming parents, it is sure to up the conflict ante for every couple. Small wonder that *Newsweek* magazine decreed parenting "The Toughest Job You'll Ever Love." Or, of greater concern, that the National Marriage Project at Rutgers University reached the chilling conclusion that "children seem to be a growing impediment for the happiness of marriages." [12]

Husbands and wives disagree about parenting in innumerable ways. They may accuse one another of being too strict or too lenient, of not being involved enough with the children or of being too involved. Some couples argue about feel-ing undermined by the other parent when setting limits on the kids. Some feel that the other is competing for the children's love.

If both of you are deeply invested in how your kids are raised, you're going to fight about things like time-outs, toys, curfews, hairstyles, clothing choices, and the best way to make your daughter's first date sweat. But that's okay—it means you're both dedicated to the same goal. How you work together to achieve that goal is where the friction comes in.

Jim and Cassidy, married fourteen years, had the same daily dispute: they fought about how to get their three children out the door every morning. First, they argued about how to rouse the kids. Jim believed they should learn responsibility by setting their own alarm clocks and getting up themselves. Cassidy insisted on waking each child herself. Then came the battle over breakfast. Jim thought grabbing fruit to eat on the way to school was fine. Cassidy wanted a sit-down meal. Rattled by

> To observe people in conflict is a necessary part of a child's education. It helps him to understand and accept his own occasional hostilities and to realize that differing opinions need not imply an absence of love.
>
> MILTON R. SAPIRSTEIN

their parents' bickering, the kids—two girls, twelve and ten, and an eight-year-old boy—created distractions, refused to listen, dawdled, and nearly always missed the school bus. Then Jim typically shouted that they needed to understand consequences and should walk. Cassidy always overruled him and drove the kids so they wouldn't be late for class. What might have been just an ordinary set of complications in other households became an obstinate conflict that led to innumerable bad fights.

How to Minimize Parenting Prizefights

The solution for nearly any parenting conflict is found in getting on the same page and presenting a unified front. Otherwise, your kids play you against each other and add fuel to the parenting fire. Conflict decreases as teamwork increases. It may not be easy to agree with your spouse on the rules and standards you are willing to enforce with your kids. That's why the first order of business is to iron out differences behind closed doors. This was the fatal mistake of Jim and Cassidy. They tried to solve their parenting squabbles in the moment—while the kids enjoyed the show. The time for presenting your ideas and negotiating trade-offs is when the two of you are alone. Once you reach agreement, stick together. When parents present a united front, there's no room for recriminating I-told-you-so's.

If you can't come up with a compromise that works, it's time to try turn-taking. This is a remarkably effective way to resolve stubborn, repetitious parenting clashes. You simply allow your spouse to be temporarily in charge of handling a contentious matter in whatever way he or she sees fit. Your job is to observe without negative comment, convey a spirit of togetherness, and save any discussion for your next meeting. Couples who try this for two weeks, where one parent gets his say one week and the other gets the next, will see a marked difference.

> The quickest way for a parent to get a child's attention is to sit down and look comfortable.
> **LANE OLINGHOUSE**

Here's how this could work for Jim and Cassidy. For the first week, Jim decides how to wake the children, what they eat for breakfast, and what to do if they miss the bus. Cassidy bites her tongue and conveys as much support as she can muster. She gets her turn the second week while Jim supports her. The result? The kids wake up to a day without bickering. They'll try to get their parents to fight, but it won't work. More likely than not, Jim and Cassidy will see the good and bad in each of their approaches and will mesh the best of both systems in the third week. The turn-taking experiment breaks the deadlock and clears the air for a new start with Mom and Dad on the same team.

If you wonder about what kind of effect these frequent changes in procedure will have on the children, a better question is, what will be the effect on them if nothing is done? They already live with the confusing chaos of divided parental authority. Three weeks of rule changes can hardly do them more harm and, in fact, will end up doing them some great good. When they see their parents unite on a consistently enforced pattern, it will greatly increase order and security in their world.

We have one more suggestion for frazzled parents. It's something we instituted in our marriage soon after our first son was born, and we still do it all these years later. We call it the daily check-in. It's what big business calls regular team meetings—a procedure employed for decades to keep workers happy, productive, and in the loop. Your meetings, however, will be more fun than listening to Steve from accounting go over last month's sales numbers. One version of this spousal meeting is called High-Low. Sometime in the evening you simply check in with your mate by telling each other your high moment and low moment for the day. That's it. Just a couple of minutes does the trick. As quick and easy as it is, sharing this bit of info keeps the two of you up-to-date and on the same team.

HIGH-LOW

Sharing the peak and pit of your day is easier than ever. You may have a desire to do this daily with each other, but that doesn't always ensure that you will do it. *High-Low* on your smartphone or tablet does. Not only does it gently remind you to do this brief exercise together, it helps you to communicate your high and low more effectively. In fact, if circumstances dictate, the two of you don't even have to be in the same vicinity to put this into practice. It works great even when you're apart.

FIGHTING THROUGH HOUSEWORK

When women began to enter the workforce in large numbers in the 1970s, it seemed logical that one day husbands and wives would divide making money and taking care of the home in a fifty-fifty split. As it turns out, that assumption was a little naive. Gender norms for who does what inside the home are more deeply ingrained than sociologists thought.

Women joining the workforce soon faced a new challenge: getting their husbands to chip in more with the housework. That sometimes led to fights. No. That almost always led to fights. Women whose husbands ran the dishwasher at night and emptied it in the morning without being asked were lucky exceptions. The man who cleared the table by dumping the dishes into the sink and walking away was the norm. That unhappy norm led to a lot of married women asking, pleading, goading, or even yelling for a little more help around the home.

Husbands and wives have never before had workloads as similar to each other's as they have today. Yet couples who split housework down the middle are as hard to find as the great white whale. Surveys show that 73 percent of women say they do more than 50 percent of the housework. When asked about their motivation for doing more than their share, the most common reason cited is, "If I don't do it, it won't get done."

Is this martyr complex accurate? Do husbands really leave their wives high and dry on the home front these days? A recent study published in the *Journal of Family Psychology* followed thirty couples in which each partner worked outside the home. All had at least one child between eight and ten years old. The authors found that about 30 percent of women spent their after-work time doing chores, compared with 20 percent of men. About 19 percent of men engaged in leisure activity after work, compared with only 11 percent of women.[13] No doubt about it, more married women than married men tend to work a second shift at home.

One reason for husband-wife inequity in housework occurs because of what we call the "threshold level." In almost all marriages, one partner will have a higher threshold of tolerance for undone work than the other. The person with the lowest tolerance does more of the work because he or she can't stand to see the trash unemptied, the floor unswept, or the pile of dishes stacked in the sink. The partner with the higher mess threshold may not even notice these undone tasks until they are pointed out.

In the past a high male threshold for undone housework mattered little because stay-at-home wives took care of such things while the husband was at work. But now things are different. Never before have married men carried so much domestic responsibility with so few role models. Findings revealing the widespread belief that working mothers have it the worst—a belief that engenders an enormous amount

> Love is the thing that enables a woman to sing while she mops up the floor after her husband has walked across it in his barn boots.
> HOOSIER FARMER

of conflict between spouses—is simply not the open-and-shut case it once was. Plenty of research shows that men do indeed *want* to be helpful around the house. A national survey of 963 fathers conducted by Boston College's Center for Work and Family found that 57 percent of men agreed with the statement, "In the past three months, I have not been able to get everything done at home each day because of my job." Job responsibilities often increase men's hours, making it virtually impossible to equalize the responsibilities of maintaining a home. The bottom line is that nobody is saying the chore wars between couples are easy. Even if both partners do not work full time, tension involving housework can be palpable.

How to Call a Truce in Your Chore Wars

So what's a couple to do? How can we keep conflict to a minimum when it comes to housework? The answer, ironic as it may seem, may be found in the workplace. They call it a "division of labor." A husband and wife, like two divisions of a company, bring assets, abilities, and interests to the table. By figuring out which person has the comparative advantage in a range of tasks, from doing dishes to walking the dog, a couple can decide who should specialize in what. This eliminates the fifty-fifty fallacy.

Let's face it, most housework fights come about because one spouse is keeping score. That's a bad idea. The scales of marriage are always in flux, and you're only setting yourselves up for turmoil if you've installed a figurative scoreboard in your relationship. Using the division of labor approach does away with all that.

Trina, for example, is better and faster than Dan at both doing the dishes and tidying up around the house. In fact, she does it in half the time it takes him. Given this fact, does it make sense for Dan to do either of these tasks? Not really. What does make sense is for Dan to refresh the water bowl for their pet and prepare their child's room for bedtime. He's also quicker at organizing and tracking their finances. He does it in half the time it would take Trina. He's also pretty good at ironing his own shirts.

> The obvious and fair solution to the housework problem is to let men do the housework for, say, the next six thousand years, to even things up.
> **DAVE BARRY**

You get the idea. It's simple. Quit trying to divide the household chores down the middle. Marriage is lived best when you're not trying to balance the scales. Instead, each of you can take on the tasks where you have the advantage. The collective gain from doing what you specialize in helps both of you to reclaim moments you've been missing together. It also helps you to minimize the casualty count in your personal chore wars. So put away the calculator, quit keeping score, and do a little give-and-take based on what *really* works best rather than what you think *should* work best.

One more thing: to squash the chore wars before they start, try a little gratitude. Why? Over time, the person who completes a chore becomes the expert on that task, and it's seen as his or her job. It becomes expected. That's when the thank-yous dry up and household skirmishes start. Studies show that partners who feel appreciated have less resentment over labor imbalances and more satisfaction with their marriage.[14] So if you're liberal with gratitude for your spouse's contribution around the house, you're sure to keep conflict to a minimum.

RESOLVING CHORE WARS

Are you battling over who does what around the house more often than you'd like? *Resolving Chore Wars* on your smartphone or tablet will help you explore your personal division of labor by examining what you'd both like to see happen and how you can get closer to your dream scenario.

KEEP THE CORE IN MIND

A couple, married for sixty years, loved each other deeply and had shared everything throughout their life. They had not kept any secrets from one another, except for one thing. When they got married, the wife put a small shoebox in the top of her closet and asked her husband never to look inside of it and never to ask questions about its contents.

For sixty years the man honored his wife's request. In fact, he forgot about the box until a day when his wife grew gravely ill. The doctors were sure she would not recover, so the man, putting his wife's affairs in order, remembered that box. He got it down and brought it to her at the hospital. He asked her if now they might open it. She agreed. They opened the box, and inside were two crocheted dolls and a roll of money totaling ninety-five thousand dollars. The man was astonished.

"Honey, what's this all about?" he asked.

"Before we married," the wife confessed, "my grandmother told me that when a woman and her husband got into an argument with one another, they should work hard to reconcile. But if they were unable to reconcile, she should simply keep her mouth shut and crochet a doll."

The man was deeply touched. He looked at the two crocheted dolls in the box and was amazed that in sixty years of marriage, they apparently had been unable to reconcile only two conversations. Tears came to his eyes, and he felt even more deeply in love with this woman.

"So what's with this?" he asked, holding up the roll of money.

"Well, every time I crocheted a doll," his wife said, "I sold it to a local craft shop for five dollars."

We all find our own ways of coping with conflict. In this chapter we've given you fresh approaches to dealing with the five most common places where couples tend to get embroiled in tension: money, sex, work, parenting, and housework. These strategies are proven and effective. But don't for a moment think they are the *only* ways to minimize the problems surrounding these hot topics. Maybe crocheting dolls isn't the answer for you. As long as you keep the **CORE** of a good fight in mind, you'll be able to come up with other effective methods that work well for the two of you.

> Love one another and you will be happy. It's as simple and as difficult as that.
> **MICHAEL LEUNIG**

FOR REFLECTION

- Of all these common issues couples fight about—money, sex, work, parenting, and housework—which two top your list and how frequently does each of them come up?

- Do you agree that most financial fights are not about finances but more accurately about power, security, values, and dreams? Consider your last money squabble. Which one of these real issues was it really about?

- Which topic do you feel the two of you fight best about? Why? How has fighting through this particular topic made your marriage stronger?

★ CHAPTER 9 ★

THE FIGHT THAT CAN SAVE YOUR MARRIAGE

Marriage is our last, best chance to grow up.

JOSEPH BARTH

IN THE ROMANTIC COMEDY *Just Married,* Tom Leezak, played by Ashton Kutcher, is a blue-collar radio reporter when he meets Sarah McNerney, the daughter of a millionaire, played by Brittany Murphy. The unlikely couple falls in love and gets married.[1]

They fly to Europe for what turns into an excruciatingly long honeymoon. An accident en route to their hotel forces them to sleep overnight in a car that is stuck in a snowbank. Once in their hotel, they're kicked out when an accidental fire breaks out in their room. With no vacancies in any other hotels, the couple is forced to stay at a filthy boardinghouse.

Tensions between the two escalate. In Florence, Sarah wants to visit churches and museums, but Tom is content to hang out in an American bar and watch the Dodgers on satellite television. To make matters worse, Sarah's ex-boyfriend shows up on a business trip and attempts to spend time with her.

The couple returns from their honeymoon seething with anger and convinced they made a terrible mistake in getting married. Both agree that they want a divorce. Sarah's family hovers around her in their gated mansion while Tom seeks solace from Kyle, his old roommate.

Convinced he doesn't have what it takes to measure up to Sarah's wealthy family's expectations (or hers), Tom retreats to his dad's house. The scene opens with Tom seated on the couch next to his father in the family room. He and his dad are watching a baseball game on television.

His dad asks, "Gonna tell me what you're chewing on?"

Tom responds without looking at his dad: "I just don't know if love is enough anymore."

"What do you mean, 'enough'?" his father questions.

"I mean, even if Sarah and I do love each other, maybe we need more time to get to know each other." Tom's eyes nervously dart toward the ground.

The father looks at his son with compassion and replies, "So what you're saying here is a couple of bad days in Europe and it's over? It's time to grow up, Tommy. Some days your mother and me loved each other. Other days we had to work at it."

He reaches down to the coffee table and picks up a family photo album. "You never see the hard days in a photo album, but those are the ones that get you from one happy snapshot to the next. I'm sorry your honeymoon stunk, but that's what you got dealt. Now you gotta work through it. Sarah doesn't need a guy with a fat wallet to make her happy. I saw how you love this girl, how you two lit each other up. She doesn't need any more security than that."

> How bold one gets when one is sure of being loved.
> SIGMUND FREUD

Grateful for his dad's advice, Tom glances toward his father and says, "Thanks."

The scene dissolves to Kyle and Tom in conversation. His old roommate asks, "Is it over?" To which Tom replies, "Not even close!"

Marriage, over time, is made up of more hard days than most of us can count. After all, we fall in love with a dream and marry a fantasy. We can't help it. Our hopes are high and our outlook is at the peak of optimism. Our partner's flaws are hidden deep in the background. Our challenges haven't even registered. Because this person loves us and we love this person, we feel connected and completed.

But eventually—though not typically on the honeymoon—things start to go badly. The illusion begins to fade, and we start seeing less-than-appealing qualities in our mate we hadn't seen before. Even traits we once admired begin to grate on our nerves. We feel our partner isn't loving us and caring for us as promised. Since we're no longer getting what we need, we try to coerce our mate into caring through criticism, intimidation, shame, withdrawal, crying, anger—whatever works. Of course, our partner is doing the same with us. The power struggle starts and the bickering begins.

Why? The answer is often deeper than you might think.

APPEARANCES CAN BE DECEIVING

Someone said that when the wedding march begins, a bride sees three things: the aisle, the altar, and him. From that time on her motto is, "I'll alter him." When the alterations don't take, the result is disillusionment, difficulty, and conflict.

The idea of changing our spouse after we marry engenders plenty of jokes for comedians, but the sobering truth is that we have an even deeper hope. Deep down, we want marriage to change *us*. We want it to change our personal story. At a level we're often unaware of, we want our marriage to make up for something in our life that we can't always identify. That something stems from our childhood.

As every fifth grader who's studied icebergs can tell you, appearances can be deceiving. We see only a small bit of ice on the surface while the largest part lurks below. We may say, for example, that money struggles are the source of our conflicts, but the real issue, the bigger issue, is often much deeper.

If you are continually fighting about unwashed dishes, says Harville Hendrix, author of *Getting the Love You Want*, "It's not about the dishes. There's a symbolic connection that triggers a deeper feeling."[2] According to Hendrix, intense and recurring arguments are a good indicator that one or both partners have unresolved childhood pain such as abandonment, rejection, smothering, shame, or helplessness.

Think of it this way. When you get married, the hurts and unmet needs from your childhood are subtly activated, and you believe you've found the person who will help you heal those long-standing childhood wounds and meet those unmet needs. Of course, you probably do not consciously acknowledge this. But you married this person because he or she brought a sense of wholeness and completion to your life like nobody you've ever known. You believe this person is going to make up for and instill in you everything you've been lacking. Your doubts about your competency, your fears of being smothered, your worries about abandonment—they'll all be made better because you've married a person who will make them so. That's your unconscious hope.

> Our wounds are often the openings into the best and most beautiful part of us.
> DAVID RICHO

But when your partner lets you down by being depressed, critical, unavailable, unreliable, neglectful—or whatever caused your hurt and pain when you were young—it strikes a nerve. It activates an alarm by reminding you of a similar moment in childhood when you experienced wounding from a caregiver. It's like a fighter who has an unhealed broken rib. If you punch him in a particular place on his rib cage, it's going to cut like a knife.

Some of us can quickly identify our unhealed wounds. If your mom or dad was an alcoholic or emotionally abusive, for example, you're likely to identify that alarm readily. But even if you came from a stable and relatively healthy home, you'll have painful issues that stem from childhood. Nobody comes out of childhood unscathed. No matter how loving your parents were or how hard they tried, they weren't perfect. Invariably, they failed to meet some of your essential needs, which left you with an emotional wound. All parents, from the worst to the best, invariably rejected some aspects of their offspring, either through criticism ("Don't act that way") or inattention (for example, ignoring our anger or ambition or even certain interests and talents). Thus each of us has various layers of denial, emotional dishonesty, buried trauma, and unfulfilled needs as a result of our early years. The more wounded we were as a child, the more pressure we put on our partner to help us heal.

Here's the bottom line. We form our ideas about relationships in connection to our parents, and when our needs aren't met, we cry, sulk, or even rebel. If we still don't get what we want, we carry an internal, invisible wound. To avoid being wounded again, we become defensive. We might withdraw emotionally, for example, or we might escalate our demands and get angry. As the saying goes, "Hurt people hurt people."

SPOTTING THE TENDER SPOTS

Having this tool on your smartphone or tablet will not only help you point to the bruises and tender places that are especially vulnerable during a fight, but it will also help you to spot those places in your partner as well. Why is this important? Because the more you understand each other's bruises, the better you can protect and love one another.

OUR STORIES

When you identify the pain or unmet need that keeps getting triggered in your marriage, you've identified the fight that can also save it. To show you what we mean, allow each of us to share our stories.

Leslie's Story

My conception came as a complete surprise to my parents. As a young bride in her late teens, my mom was diagnosed with juvenile diabetes. The doctors counseled her never to have children because of the severe health risks involved for both her and the baby. My dad had enrolled in a doctoral program, which required a commitment that prevented him from holding a job while studying. My mom, therefore, had happily accepted a teaching position to support them while he completed his studies. To their great shock and surprise, an illness my mom was experiencing turned out to be a pregnancy, requiring her to resign her teaching job. Consequently, my dad was forced to drop his doctoral studies.

The doctors were so pessimistic about the pregnancy (and my mom so ill) that my parents didn't pick out a name or decorate a nursery. They just endured the months of waiting for the inevitable. So my birth and survival were both an unexpected miracle and a life-altering reality.

The story of my birth initiates the script of my life and reveals the scars of my soul. In some ways, I have been gifted with a deep sense of significance, seeing my life as an unexpected miracle of God's grace. In other ways, I have been painfully aware that I am in no way a miracle and that no matter how hard I tried, I couldn't erase the pain of my mom's chronic, debilitating illness. Nor could I fill the gaps in my father's soul that eventually led to my parents' divorce in the thirty-fifth year of their marriage.

One of my most vivid early memories is from a time when I was just two years old. My mom went into a diabetic coma, and my dad was away on a trip. I was alone with her and failed to get her to drink orange juice (one thing I had been trained to do for Mom if she needed help). Of course, when people are in a coma, they cannot swallow. My last resort was to dial the operator (in those days, 0 on a rotary phone). When the operator answered, she scolded me, saying, "Little girl, quit playing on your phone," and hung up. I thought my mom was dying, and my efforts to save her had failed. Later, my father came home. Mom was revived and restored completely.

The quest to prevent Mom's pain and my mission to heal Dad's dashed hopes defined my childhood, mostly in ways I was unaware of until I became a young adult. My woundedness comes from the feeling that I disappointed my parents. My very existence had endangered my mother's health and prevented my dad's chosen career, not that either of them would say that or even think it. In fact, they would both tell you how proud they are of their daughter. Yet, early on, I carried an abiding sense of grief that I could have done more to make their lives better, but I couldn't perform miracles.

> I suppose that since most of our hurts come through relationships so will our healing, and I know that grace rarely makes sense for those looking in from the outside.
>
> W. PAUL YOUNG

Starting life not just as an only child but as a "miracle" child established a role for me that I unconsciously work hard to maintain even to this day. I have a tireless need to be a person worthy of devotion, affirmation, and affection. In short, I have an unconscious need to be my husband's miracle.

Of course, that's an impossibility. I know that. It's a ridiculous notion. Admittedly irrational. But I often cling to it, fearing I might lose my husband's approval because I let him down. As you might imagine, this fear kicks in with the slightest criticism. In fact, it sometimes causes me to see criticism where it doesn't exist, even on superficial matters. If Les is drinking his morning orange juice and says something like, "I think there's something sticky on this countertop," I take it personally. I hear him saying, "You're failing as a wife by not keeping this countertop clean." Of course, he means no such thing. My reaction does not come from trying to win a prize for having a shipshape kitchen; I have far more at stake than a dirty counter. I fear losing my husband's approval. A little, innocent comment is all it takes for my childhood wound to be exposed and my defenses to mount. "That's from John's pancakes," I might say with an edge in my voice. "Just give me a minute to clean it." So I protect my wound—even from such an insignificant comment—by quickly shielding it from any further pain.

> A good marriage is the union of two good forgivers.
> RUTH BELL GRAHAM

Do you think this tendency of mine might exacerbate our conflicts? Of course it does. But let's hear Les's story now, and then we'll both tell you how our wounds exacerbate each other.

Les's Story

I grew up in an upper-middle-class home with two loving parents. I had a wonderful childhood, mostly in Boston, with summers on the coast of Maine. If you took a good look at my childhood, you'd say I have nothing to complain about—and you'd be right. In fact, I count the home I came from to be among my greatest blessings. I don't know how I could have had more loving, supportive, and invested parents.

So what kind of woundedness could I possibly have from childhood? At first, the very thought of such a wound seemed absurd to me. But I had a professor in graduate school who pushed me to give it serious study. And I did. Now, many years later, I can sum it up in a word: abandonment. Even as I write that word I cringe. Mom and Dad never neglected me or left me uncared for. Never. They wouldn't think of it. But they did sometimes leave me—with Grandma, baby-sitters, and other families. Their work required a lot of travel, and that meant leaving.

Was I traumatized by it? My impulse is to say not at all. But the fact remains that I spent a good chunk of my growing-up years seeing Mom and Dad leave me. I recall a stay with Grandma when I was just a toddler. I cried for my parents, and she told me that no matter how loud I cried, they couldn't hear me. I remember crying routinely when my mom dropped me off at preschool. While Mom and Dad were on the road, I felt desperately alone during more than a few sleepovers with families I barely knew. As a first or second grader, I distinctly remember begging my mom to stay with me during my swimming lessons. She did it because I insisted, even though she was the only parent sitting poolside. Some kids might have been embarrassed. I was relieved.

In my teen years, Mom and Dad talked to me about attending a boarding school. We toured the grounds and met with some administrators. I took a few tests and was ready to enroll that autumn— until the family of my best friend, Greg Smith, talked to my parents about letting me live with them for the school year instead.

Greg and I had met while in the third grade in Boston, and it was an instant friendship. We lived two blocks from each other and did everything together—rode bicycles everywhere, played endless hours of basketball and hockey, fished in nearby ponds, and had countless sleepovers at each other's houses. We were nearly inseparable until both of our families moved from Boston within a year of each other—mine to Chicago, his to Kansas City.

So when the Smiths offered to let me live with them while going to school in Kansas City, I was thrilled. To be reunited with my best buddy was fantastic. But once again, it meant saying good-bye for a while to Mom and Dad. Of course, I talked with them on the phone most days. Dad even read my schoolbooks along with me so we could discuss them together. They came to KC frequently, and I was often back home in Chicago with them. We expressed affection and always said, "I love you." But for three years of my adolescence, I spent more time with the Smith family than with my own. I don't resent it. In fact, those were great years with wonderful and hilarious memories. So to say I have a woundedness due to abandonment sounds more severe than circumstances may seem to warrant. But I suppose it's the best way to capture the lingering effect of my childhood experience.

WHEN TWO WOUNDS COLLIDE

It was Sunday, and Les and I were delighted that we had secured second-row seats on the right side of the church sanctuary, which happens to be the piano side of the platform. In our fast-growing church it's always a challenge to find a seat. As I was preparing my heart for worship, Les had been paying close attention to a member of the worship band who had strolled over to the piano and soulfully played some beautiful hymns and choruses as a prelude to the service. I was relishing the music too, and it was then that Les leaned over and whispered something about our two boys not practicing their piano regularly. We were throwing our money away on the lessons, he said, and if things didn't change, we should just get rid of the piano.

From my perspective, there was a lot of energy behind the statement. Les has always regretted that he did not master the piano as a boy, and he wanted to give his sons the gift of making music. Seeing the worship leader play the piano a few feet from us that Sunday morning triggered something in Les, and he communicated his frustration there and then.

My eyes immediately welled up with tears. It seemed to me that he was indicting my parenting skills and issuing an unfair ultimatum. I felt that Les was telling me I was a failure. It seemed that he was not only blaming me but also punishing both the boys and me by threatening to get rid of the piano.

I began to wallow in self-pity as I mulled over all my escalating homework pressures, church commitments, and our busy professional life. Then, on top of all that, he had to pile on the natural resistance our boys felt to practicing the piano. Anger began to mount. How could he be so insensitive as to say this to me in church, where I had made myself vulnerable and hoped to share an intimate moment of worship with my husband? How could he say such a thing at all? I wanted the same thing for our boys that Les wanted—for them to enjoy playing the piano someday instead of facing regrets over their failure to learn music.

> The words of the reckless pierce like swords, but the tongue of the wise brings healing.
> PROVERBS 12:18

As the church service started, we shot each other a couple of pointed text messages. Les felt he was just expressing his concerns, and it didn't matter if it was at church. By nature, he is a "do it now" person, and so he addressed the issue while it was on his mind.

But because I read his comment as criticism, because I took it personally, because I felt that I was letting him down, I withdrew. I shut down. From Les's perspective, I abandoned him. I rubbed salt in his childhood wound, which only made him more frustrated and angry. Here we were, both feeling distanced and hurt after just a brief moment of conversation in a place where we'd come to align our spirits with each other and with God.

That's what happens when two wounds collide. There's a synergistic effect that spirals a couple into a conflict and causes it to become deeper than it should. It's all because the human brain records and keeps track of behaviors that hinder us from getting what we need to feel protected and loved. These behaviors get recorded, right from the start, on neural networks that stay with us. That's why understanding our early wounds is critically important to helping us fight a good fight.

Unresolved childhood pain, whether it be abandonment, rejection, smothering, shame, or helplessness, is almost certain to resurface in your marriage. Whether or not your early years were traumatic, you, like all the rest of us, come into your current relationship as an adult with some painful residue from your childhood.

THE ULTIMATE DEATH MATCH

When you're not aware of how the pain from your childhood gets replayed and exacerbated in conflicts as a married adult, those childhood scenarios inevitably repeat themselves with the same devastating consequences. The trauma you experienced gets reignited, whether it's your fear of abandonment, rejection, shame, helplessness, or whatever. Heated conflict ensues, and you resort to defensive childish tactics. But once you face facts and recognize how these early unmet needs play into your current relationship, you start to grow. You mature. "It's crucial to accept the hard truth that incompatibility is the norm for relationships," says Harville Hendrix. "Conflict is a sign that the psyche is trying to survive, to heal by stretching out of its defenses."[3]

Coming to self-awareness is the greatest step you can take in correcting what has gone wrong in the past. It allows you to replace your usual defensive routine of crying or anger or withdrawal with the CORE qualities of a good fight: Cooperation, Ownership, Respect, and Empathy. Armed with the kind of self-awareness that explains your own pain, you are better equipped to drop your guard, cooperate, take responsibility, show respect, and empathize with the pain of your partner. It is impossible to practice these CORE qualities if you're unconsciously trying to get your partner to meet your unmet needs or heal your hidden hurts. When that's your focus, you can't help but be guarded and consumed with your own pain. You lack the maturity to look beyond it and fight a good fight.

That's why we call this fight—the one you have with your childhood pain—the ultimate death match. The name sounds grim and fatal, but don't worry. The only thing it's meant to kill is your immature fighting with your mate. That's what you want to put an end to. This fight, therefore, is not with your mate at all. It is with yourself. Your goal is to put to death that self-defensive reflex to protect that

> All those "and they lived happily ever after" fairy-tale endings need to be changed to "and they began the very hard work of making their marriages happy."
> **LINDA MILES**

painful element within you that turns every disagreement with your mate into World War III. At the risk of oversimplifying, this is a fight that can be won with two good roundhouse punches.

Punch 1: Retire the Victim Role

There's an old tale about a farmer who sees a man on a horse galloping swiftly along the road. The farmer calls out, "Hey, where are you going?" The rider turns around and shouts back, "Don't ask me. Ask my horse." That's the general response of a victim. Like this rider, victims feel utterly helpless. Self-pity, defeat, and helplessness pervade their thinking. Their common refrain is, "There's nothing I can do about it."

But if you're serious about maturing, you must give up your identity as a victim and let go of whatever payoff you've been getting from hopelessness and despair. The payoff might be attention or validation. It might be the comfortable lethargy of inaction because you're convinced there's nothing you can do. Whatever your secondary gain, you need to give it up to break the martyr mentality and begin taking responsibility for your life. You're not trapped by fate, destiny, or God.

"No matter what you have been through, you're still here," says philanthropist Steve Maraboli. "You may have been challenged, hurt, betrayed, beaten, and discouraged, but nothing has defeated you. You are still here! You have been delayed but not denied. You are not a victim, you are a victor."

Playing the victim is a choice, and you can choose differently. Being a victim is a thought, and you can think differently. It's a process, which means it won't happen overnight, but the process can start today. You can ask God, your true source of power, to help you take on a genuine sense of self.

Punch 2: Help Your Partner Find Healing Too

An ancient tale describes a young girl who was walking through a meadow when she saw a butterfly impaled on a thorn. She carefully released the butterfly, which started to fly away but came back after it had changed into a beautiful fairy. "For your kindness," the fairy told the little girl, "I will grant your fondest wish."

The little girl thought for a moment and replied, "I want to be happy." The fairy leaned toward her, whispered in her ear, and then suddenly vanished.

As the child grew, no one in the land was happier than she. Whenever anyone asked her for the secret of her happiness, she would only smile and say, "I listened to a good fairy."

As she grew old, the neighbors were afraid the fabulous secret might die with her. "Tell us, please," they begged. "Tell us what the fairy said."

The lovely old lady simply smiled and said, "She told me that everyone, no matter how apparently self-sufficient, has need of me!"

It's the same secret you need to hear about your spouse. Your mate has great need of you, just as you have great need of your mate. As paradoxical as it may sound, the healing you're looking for from your childhood wounds is found in helping your partner heal his or her wounds. It's a shared journey of mutual growth. In helping your spouse reclaim the loss and wounded part he or she has been protecting, you'll

> The single biggest problem in communication is the illusion that it has taken place.
> GEORGE BERNARD SHAW

discover a symbiotic healing of your own. You'll find your own defenses relaxing as you see them mellow in your mate. As you try to understand and empathize with your partner's unmet needs, you'll find that the effort is reciprocated. Vulnerability begets vulnerability.

THE PRICE WE PAY FOR DEEPER INTIMACY

Nobody gets over past wounds quickly. It's a process, and the process will likely be fraught with conflict. But the payoff for the conflict can be a deeper level of intimacy. When you fight a good fight, you use the tension and trouble to bring the two of you closer together.

Every relationship goes through four stages. The first stage is *false relationship*. Remember when the two of you first started dating? You didn't try to be as genuine and real as possible. Quite the contrary. You tried to manage the impression you were making by dressing a certain way and talking about certain topics so your partner would like you. The relationship was far from authentic. In fact, it was about an inch deep. There really wasn't much to it. Neither of you knew the other as a real person. Not yet.

That process of knowing begins in full force once you enter the second stage of the relationship: *chaos*. This stage is every bit as tumultuous as it sounds. Why? Because this is where you start to get real.

The authenticity that emerges in this stage throws the relationship off balance. Your true opinions come through. You start to speak your mind. You disagree, and conflicts occur. It can get intense, and you can lose your equilibrium. It can even cause you to call the relationship into question. But this scary stage is essential if you are ever to be authentic.

Chaos gives way to a better place when you enter the third stage of relationship called *emptiness*. By emptiness we do not mean some kind of existential void. It's the capacity we have as human beings to empty ourselves of our need to change another person. This is not easy, primarily because most of us want others to do things the way we want them done. It doesn't matter whether it's our boss or a driver on the freeway or the person we married, we possess a strong human drive to have people conform to *our* ways. But when we empty ourselves of our need to change our spouse, something almost mystical begins to happen: the thing that irritates us, the quirky thing the other does that caused the fight, can become the very thing that endears that person to us.

> A wedding anniversary is the celebration of love, trust, partnership, tolerance, and tenacity. The order varies for any given year.
> PAUL SWEENEY

Emptiness—the ability to empty yourself of your desire to change your mate—builds a bridge into the fourth stage of relationship. This is the stage where we all long to be: *genuine relationship*. This is where you can relax and be yourself, knowing that you are still accepted and loved, not because you are perfect, but in spite of your imperfections. This is where your guard comes down and wounds find healing. In *genuine relationship* you are authentic and vulnerable, and you are still accepted for who you are. No pretense. The relationship is no longer an inch deep. It is oceans deep.

Note that you never get to *genuine relationship* without traveling through *chaos*. In fact, you may often visit *chaos* again and again before you cross the bridge of *emptiness* and enjoy the comfort of *genuine relationship*. This is why we say, "Conflict is the price we pay for a deeper level of intimacy."

FOUR STAGES OF RELATIONSHIP

Your relationship is constantly changing. The longer you're together, the more it enters, exits, and reenters various stages. The more accurately you can identify those stages in your relationship, the better you become at navigating them. This tool on your smartphone or tablet will help you gain further insight into your ever-changing relationship and apply the CORE principles to each stage of change.

TOGETHER FOREVER

The 1997 movie *As Good as It Gets* is a comedy about an obsessive-compulsive author, Melvin Udall, played by Jack Nicholson.[4] Melvin offends everyone he meets, but he becomes enamored with Carol Connelly, a struggling waitress played by Helen Hunt. She has seen Melvin at his worst, yet she agrees to meet him at a fancy restaurant for a date.

Carol arrives at the restaurant feeling out of place and ill at ease as the staff waits on her hand and foot. The other patrons of the restaurant are impeccably attired, but Carol wears a simple red dress, making her feel more insecure.

Melvin sees Carol and waves her over to his table. When she approaches, he hits an all-time low. "This restaurant!" he says, "they make me buy a new outfit and let you in wearing a housedress." Carol is stunned and hurt by his crassly insensitive insult, but she knows that, with Melvin, it's part of the package.

She looks him in the eye and says, "Pay me a compliment, Melvin. I need one now."

Melvin responds, "I've got a great compliment." What could he possibly say to undo the thoughtless comment he had just delivered?

But Melvin surprises us by delivering one of the most romantic lines in big-screen history. This deeply flawed and socially challenged man, with all his wounds and debilitating hang-ups, looks at Carol with all the kindness and sincerity his shriveled heart can muster and says, "Carol, you make me want to be a better man."

And she does. That's the payoff of a relationship made up of two wounded people. Bright glimmers of maturity shine through even in the midst of chaos. That's the course of love between two imperfect people, mismatched like every other couple on the planet but making each other want to be better. They do their best to find their footing, often losing their balance. But each time they fall, they stand up again to fight the good fight.

> There are three words that save a marriage, and they're not, "I love you." They are: "Maybe you're right."
>
> ANONYMOUS

Together.

FOR REFLECTION

- How would you describe any wounds you carry from childhood? How do you see them impacting your marriage relationship today?

- As you consider the four stages of relationship—*false relationship, chaos, emptiness,* and *genuine relationship*—what stage would you say the two of you are in right now? Why?

- How would you rate your growth and your healing in relationship to the wounds or pain you carry from childhood? Do you feel that you are making progress? Why or why not?

★ CONCLUSION ★
KEEPING THE PEACE

IN 1937 A RESEARCHER at Harvard University began a study on what factors contribute to human well-being and happiness. The research team selected 268 Harvard students who seemed healthy and well adjusted to be part of what is called a longitudinal study. This means the researchers study the lives of these people not just at one point in time but rather over a period of time. In this case, the period of time was extraordinary: seventy-two years. It's one of the most in-depth and important studies of our time. With over seven decades of perspective, the study yielded a comprehensive viewpoint on what factors affect the level of health and happiness over a person's lifetime.

The study tracked an array of factors, including standard measurable items like physical exercise, cholesterol levels, marital status, the use of alcohol, smoking, education levels, and weight. It also tracked more subjective psychological factors such as how a person employs defense mechanisms to deal with the challenges of life.

Over the last forty-two years of the study, the director of the study was psychiatrist George Vaillant. In 2008 someone asked him what he had learned about human health and happiness from his years of poring over the data on these people. You would expect a complex answer from a Harvard social scientist, but he said the study showed that the secret to happiness is breathtakingly simple: "The only thing that really matters in life is your relationships."[1]

That's it: relationships. The most in-depth study ever conducted on the well-being of human beings sums up what matters most for our health and happiness with that single word. It's not surprising really. As researchers have pursued the age-old mystery of what makes people happy, what appears consistently at the top of the charts is not success, wealth, achievement, good looks, or any of those enviable assets. It's always relationships. Close ones. In fact, marriage is at the centerpiece of close human relationships, for it's in the context of marriage that our deepest needs can be met—as long as the relationship is working.

So we end where we began. No couple, no matter how loving, is immune to conflict. Fighting is as intrinsic to marriage as sex. And the goal for both is to do them well. That's why we've dedicated this book to helping you fight a good fight. Paradoxically, that is ultimately the best way to keep the peace in your marriage. Fighting well and productively comes about

> There is nothing more admirable than two people who see eye-to-eye keeping house as man and wife, confounding their enemies, and delighting their friends.
>
> **HOMER**

when you learn to practice the four **CORE** elements of a good fight. After all, the relationship you share with your spouse is well worth fighting for, because no matter how charged with frustration it may sometimes be, it is the greatest source of health and happiness you'll ever find on this planet.

★ APPENDIX ★

CONTROLLING ANGER BEFORE IT CONTROLS YOU

IT WAS KNOWN IN Hollywood as the "Mel-tdown." And it was broadcast all over the world. Mel Gibson's phone rant at Oksana Grigorieva, mother of his eight-month-old daughter, was so angry, so rage filled, that it included a death threat. So violent were his emotions and so crudely expressed—a cascade of F bombs and C words interspersed with racist and sexist insults—that professionals expressed concern for Gibson's mental health.

We want to give you a brief excerpt of the vile exchange to make a point. Be forewarned: it's harsh, crass, and crude—and we're excluding some of the ugliest parts. So feel free to skip this little transcript if you like:

> *Mel Gibson:* Stay on this phone and don't hang up on me. I have plenty of energy to drive over there. You understand me? AND I WILL! SO JUST F— LISTEN TO ME. LISTEN TO MY F— RANTING. LISTEN TO WHAT YOU DO TO ME.

Oksana Grigorieva: I didn't do anything to you.

MG: You make my life so f— difficult!

OG: Well, you know what, it's so—

MG: Why can't you be a woman who f— supports me instead of a woman that sucks off me. And just f— sucks me dry. And wants and wants. Go through this relationship if you're a good woman and you love me. I don't believe you anymore. I'm sick of your bull—! Has any relationship ever worked with you? NO!

OG: Listen to me. You don't love me because somebody who loves does not behave this way.

MG: Shut the f— up. I know I'm behaving like this because I know absolutely that you do not love me and you treat me with no consideration.

OG: One second, please. Can I please speak?

MG: I love you because I've treated you with every kindness, every consideration. You rejected...you will never be happy. F— you! Get the f— away from me! But my daughter is important! All right? Now, you have one more chance. And I mean it. Now f— go if you want, but I will give you one more chance. (Huffing with anger.) You make me wanna smoke. You f— my day up. You care about yourself.

OG: You're so selfish.

MG: When I've been so f— good to you. You f— try to destroy me.

OG: I didn't do anything. I did not do anything. This is your selfish imagination. That's bull!

MG: Shut the f— up! You should just f— smile and b— me! 'Cause I deserve it.

OG: I'm sleeping with the baby. I'm waking up every

two hours. I fell asleep because I was waiting for you
because you weren't ready to go to the Jacuzzi as
we agreed.

MG: Who the f— cares? We agreed nothing.

Gibson's raging rants, recorded by Grigorieva for her own protection, seem to go on interminably. The chilling vitriol reveals a picture of a movie star turned monster. But these rage-filled tirades also raise a provocative question: could any otherwise decent human being develop into a monster like that? Psychologists who specialize in anger say there's a familiarity to the star's fury. It's reminiscent of some marital fights nearing the breaking point. If we strip away the potty-mouthiness, is Mel Gibson all that different from some of us?

More to the point, can the same emotional intensity, the same venomous anger, be part of your fights? After all, frustrating moments in marriage can bring out the worst parts of anyone's nature. When it feels as if every-

> Whenever you are angry, be assured that it is not only a present evil, but that you have increased a habit.
> EPICTETUS

thing and everyone is conspiring against you, even your spouse, and the frustration builds inside you, is that frustration at risk of turning into rage?

It takes just one person to ruin a good fight. It can happen when one's feelings reach the tipping point, and they turn from being a long-suffering victim into an avenger who justifies any kind of fuming retaliation. Anger of this kind, when red-hot and out of control, becomes so intense and debilitating that it eliminates any possibility of maintaining a cooperative spirit. It's not about to let the overheated person take an ounce of responsibility for any wrongdoing. It certainly empties one's capacity to maintain respect or to see the other partner's perspective. In short, unmanaged anger makes it impossible to get to the **CORE** of a good fight.

So we ask the question again: when you and your spouse are fighting, are either of you especially prone to angry outbursts? Let's face it, you probably wouldn't be reading this appendix if you weren't concerned about an anger problem. Well, the hard fact is—and maybe you'll find this comforting or maybe you'll find it frightening— there are a lot of people out there who struggle with raging anger. That's why we included this appendix. It may not be for everyone, but it's vital for a wide swath of husbands and wives who know that anger is problematic for them and sometimes interferes with their ability to fight a good fight.

> An angry man opens his mouth and shuts up his eyes.
> CATO

We want to give you a new perspective on this dicey emotion of anger. As we are about to explain, it's not all bad. We'll also look at a few erroneous beliefs about anger that can trip us up. We'll help both of you understand what's going on when angry outbursts occur and what you can do to tame an angry temper. As always, we're giving you proven strategies that work for the vast majority of couples. You won't find armchair psychobabble or platitudes here.

THE GOOD, THE BAD, AND THE ANGRY

Anger, some say, is all the rage in American life. Anger dominates our political rhetoric. Incidents of road-rage violence are increasingly common. Some popular music is angry, spiked with misogynistic rants and threatening lyrics. The nightly news is replete with stories of angry explosions that go beyond the usual violent crime, like the father who shot his daughter's laptop with a handgun because she wasn't listening to him. Of course, there's also the strident bloggers, finger-pointing cablenews hosts, brawling professional athletes, bullying grade-schoolers, and Little League parents who go after umpires with veins bulging.

Anger also has a positive side. It can be either one's greatest liability or a constructive asset. Carol Tavris, author of the seminal *Anger: The Misunderstood Emotion*, explains:

> I have watched people use anger, in the name of emotional liberation, to erode affection and trust, whittle away their spirits in bitterness and revenge, diminish their dignity in years of spiteful hatred. And I watch with admiration those who use anger to probe for truth, who challenge and change the complacent injustices of life.[1]

Tavris wasn't the first to see the good in anger. Renaissance essayist Michel de Montaigne advised marshaling anger and using it wisely. He urged people to "husband their anger and not expend it at random, for that impedes its effect and weight. Heedless and continual scolding becomes a habit and makes everyone discount it."

Montaigne's advice recognizes one of the paradoxes of anger: it's often destructive, it's often a waste, but every once in a while it works. It can fuel our drive to achieve, help us maintain our self-respect, or stop the world from walking all over us. There's a tipping point, of course, where anger gets too amped up and becomes terribly destructive. Scripture clearly warns that escalating anger and venting at one another is foolish.[2]

Perhaps Aristotle said it best: "Anyone can become angry—that is easy. But to be angry with the right person, to the right degree, at the right time, for the right purpose, and in the right way—this is not easy."

Indeed it's not. Balancing the good and the bad of anger is tough. It's all too easy to fall back on Mark Twain's solution: "When angry, count to four. When very angry, swear."

That's funny, but we can do better than that.

CALL IT WHAT YOU WILL

In the 1960s an American produce importer named Frieda Caplan changed the name of the Chinese gooseberry to the kiwifruit. She got the name from New Zealand's national bird, which is also round, brown, and furry. The sales of the former gooseberry soared.

In 1977 fish merchant Lee Lantz traveled to Chile and "discovered" the toothfish, a species the locals deemed too oily to eat. Thirty years and a name change later, Chilean sea bass is so popular with American palates that it's almost on the verge of extinction.

In the year 2000 the California prune board realized the words *prune* and *laxative* were inextricably linked, which was damaging sales of their product. They solved this guilt-by-association problem by calling prunes "dried plums." Sales shot up, and in a documented focus group, people preferred the taste of dried plums to prunes.

Apparently it's not quite true that "a rose by any other name smells as sweet," which is why people have a natural bent toward renaming things to make them more palatable. But when renaming our anger in order to diminish its negativity, things can get dangerous. It leads to denial and a lack of self-awareness. We think it's more acceptable to say, "I'm not angry, I'm just frustrated" or "I'm not angry, I'm just hurt." Some of us have a hard time saying, "I'm angry!" But we must realize that anger does not always mean explosions of rage. It also comes in quieter, subtler forms and in lesser degrees. Recognizing that certain hurts and frustrations produce these less demonstrative forms of anger is an essential first step in learning to retrain your temper.

> Anybody can become angry—that is easy; but to be angry with the right person, and to the right degree, and at the right time, and for the right purpose, and in the right way—that is not within everybody's power and is not easy.
> ARISTOTLE

So if we need to admit when we have it, let's be sure we know exactly what anger is. Experts define anger as an uncomfortable emotion triggered by perceived injustice. In other words, it's related to our perception that we have been offended, wronged, denied, mistreated, opposed, or misunderstood.

Raymond Novaco of the University of California at Irvine, who since 1975 has published more professional articles than anyone on the subject, says anger involves three components:

- *Biological reactions* are felt in our body, usually starting with a rush of adrenaline, an increased heart rate and blood pressure, as well as tightening muscles.
- *Cognitive appraisals* have to do with how we perceive and think about what is making us angry. For example, we might think something that happened to us is unfair or undeserved.
- *Behavior antagonism* is the way we express our anger. We may look and sound angry, turn red, raise our voices, clam up, slam doors, storm away, or resort to any number of other actions to express our anger.

Anger has been called a sin. It has been called an emotion. Former Secretary of State Alexander Haig once called it a "management vehicle." Call it what you will, but when your biology, your thinking, and your behavior converge to warn you that you're feeling extremely upset over some perceived wrong, you're experiencing anger.

THREE MISBELIEFS ABOUT ANGER

While we're on the topic of defining anger, let's pause and lay to rest a handful of myths. Here are three important ones:

Myth: "I shouldn't hold in my anger. It's healthy to vent and let it out."

Fact: While it's true that suppressing and ignoring anger is unhealthy, venting is no better. Anger is not something you have to let out in an aggressive way in order to avoid blowing up. In fact, outbursts and tirades only fuel the fire and reinforce your mismanaged anger.

Myth: "Anger, aggression, and intimidation help me earn respect and get what I want." (Sounds like Secretary Haig's "management vehicle.")

Fact: True power doesn't come from bullying others. People may be afraid of you, but they won't respect you if you can't control yourself or handle opposing viewpoints. Your spouse, especially, will be more willing to listen to you and accommodate your needs if you communicate in a respectful way.

Myth: "I can't help myself. Anger isn't something a person can control."

Fact: You can't always control the situation you're in or how it makes you feel, but you *can* control how you express your anger. And you *can* express your anger without unleashing an unbridled tirade. Even if someone is pushing your buttons, you always have a choice about how to respond. Most of us are living proof that we can control our anger. When we're angry with someone who could hurt us in some way—say, a supervisor or an employer who could fire us—we generally control our anger to protect our interests. But when we're angry with someone without the power to damage us, we often forego control and blow up. Clearly, controlling our anger is a choice.

Anger is normal and natural. We are not responsible for being angry, but we are responsible for how we respond to and use anger once it appears. Plainly put, humans were created with a capacity to experience passionate anger. But for some quick-tempered people, anger becomes more than a human emotion. It becomes a chronic pattern of self-defeating rage.

UNDERSTANDING YOUR ANGRY SPOUSE

Before we turn to the strategies for taming your temper, we want to take a moment to speak directly to the person married to a spouse who struggles with anger. If you have never been especially prone to anger yourself, this emotion can be difficult to understand. After all, there's no obvious payoff to a fit of anger. The only results from angry episodes are hurt feelings, retaliation, or, worse, violence. Only rarely does anger result in any real resolution to the problem that started the whole thing.

So why is it that while most people let minor aggravations slide, others are prone to anger and can't contain their rage? Why are they so easily provoked? Researchers provide several answers. In experiments using deliberate provocations such as frustrating math problems and rude assistants, scientists have identified a potentially catastrophic chain reaction in these people: the brain signals the adrenal glands to dump an extra dose of stress hormones, including adrenaline, into the bloodstream. As a result, their blood boils. People who are especially prone to anger haven't learned to turn off that adrenaline shower. Rather than finding a distraction to divert them from the impulse to express rage, they are more likely to give in to it.

> If men would consider not so much where they differ, as wherein they agree, there would be far less of uncharitableness and angry feeling in the world.
> JOSEPH ADDISON

Researchers have also found that those given to chronic anger use it to defend themselves against potential pain. They may have grown up in homes where they were put down, rejected, unjustly criticized, or even abused. Their learned response to this negative environment is to protect themselves with a heavy armor of anger and aggression. They have been burned, so they fight fire with fire. They have concluded that relationships are painful, and they are not about to let others take advantage of them. Anger then becomes a way of life. It is a kind of insulation from potential psychic pain.

Another factor shaping the angry person's behavior is the modeling provided by one or both parents. A comprehensive longitudinal study of grade school children in New York revealed that aggressiveness in the parents' behavior at home is closely associated with aggressiveness in their children at school.[3] We hardly need a study, however, to tell us that children imitate their parents. If children grow up in homes where dads fly off the handle and control their families

> We often make up in wrath what we want in reason.
> WILLIAM ROUNSEVILLE ALGER

with physical and verbal abuse, it makes sense to conclude that the children will learn to use anger in the same way.

Perhaps the most clearly defined causal factor of chronic eruptions of anger is found in the person's cynical mistrust of others. They expect others to mistreat them, which puts them on the lookout for bad behavior—and they usually find it. This generates frequent anger, and that anger, combined with a lack of empathy for others, leads them to express their hostility overtly.

It may be that none of these factors is the cause of your partner's problem with anger. Everyone is unique. But on the whole, the person who is prone to angry outbursts is likely to have a combination of biological triggers, including an early history of being mistreated, a cynical attitude, and poor emotional modeling by their early caregivers.

When you take any mixture of these factors and add to it fatigue, embarrassment, or rejection, look out! You have all the ingredients for a high-octane emotional outburst.

TAMING YOUR TEMPER

Justin John Boudin, a twenty-seven-year-old man from Minnesota, pleaded guilty to fifth-degree assault charges for violently losing his temper. Here's the irony: he was on his way to an anger management class when he committed the crime.

According to the criminal complaint, Boudin was waiting at a bus stop when he started to harass a fifty-nine-year-old woman. Witnesses say he yelled at her over what he felt was a general lack of respect. When she took out her cell phone to call the police, Boudin punched her in the face. When a sixty-three-year-old man tried to stop him, Boudin hit him with a blue folder that held his anger management homework. Police tracked him down by using the papers inside.[4]

This amazing story reveals just how difficult it can be for some people to win in the struggle against unmanaged anger. But it's a struggle that can be won, and we want to give you some proven and practical steps to help you get your anger under control.

Do Nothing

Okay, we know this sounds a bit absurd, but if you don't feel as effective at diffusing anger as you would like, try this: the moment you feel your pulse quicken with anger, just stop and do nothing. This is not as easy as it may sound. Everything brewing within you wants to burst out. But if you know you don't handle your anger well, the best thing you can do at this stage is simply to stop until you have taken some time to think. Waiting a moment isn't the same as stuffing anger. Stuffing is ignoring the problem. That's not healthy, and it's not what we're recommending.

Instead, follow Thomas Jefferson's sage advice and slowly count to ten before you do anything else. As Jefferson said, if you're very angry, extend the count to one hundred. This familiar childhood admonition of counting before taking action works because it emphasizes the two key elements of anger management: time and distraction. While your mind is busy counting, it is not adding fuel to the fire of anger by stewing over whatever happened to make you angry. Counting to ten becomes an even more effective way of disarming anger if you also take a slow, deep breath between each number. Deep breathing counteracts the fight-or-flight stress reaction that underlies anger. Deliberately taking a slow, deep breath not only brings a soothing sense of relaxation, it also helps to focus your attention in the present moment.

Heed the Warning Signs

A recent survey found that 10 percent of the 2,041 U.S. adults polled were driving a car whose Check Engine light was on.[5] An alarming 50 percent of those surveyed said the light had been on for more than three months, and their cars were showing signs of an impending breakdown. The survey found that drivers had a whole litany of excuses for ignoring the light. Some turned a blind eye

> The worst-tempered people I've ever met were people who knew they were wrong.
> **WILSON MIZNER**

toward the indicator because the car seemed to be running fine. Others simply said they just didn't have time to worry about diagnostics and subsequent repairs.

Unfortunately, many of us take the same lackadaisical approach to the warning signs of anger—although we may have a better excuse than the drivers in the survey. Too many of us don't know what signs to look for. When we do, those signs become tools for helping us to avoid emotional blowups.

Signs of pre-explosive anger include the following:

- Tension—Observe what you feel in your neck. Are the muscles in your neck taut? If so, take steps to relax and get hold of yourself. Inhaling and exhaling slowly helps relax those building tensions.

- Feeling Flushed—This condition is easily perceptible because when blood circulation increases above normal, you can feel heat rising in your face. You can often feel the beat of your pulse as well. If you notice these symptoms, let them serve as signs that you are getting overheated. You need to cool down by momentarily removing yourself from the situation. You can channel the energy that's building up the heat into something productive, like going for a brisk walk or taking a trip to the gym. Or maybe all you need is a few minutes of listening to some soothing music.

- Clenched Fists—In the movies, men who are about to punch someone first clench their fists to deliver the blow. This involuntary reaction is part of an emotional process that works the same way in real life. When anger comes to the forefront, our hands can sometimes be the most obvious expression of it.

- Loud Voice—A raised voice is one of the more common and traditional ways to know someone is angry. The opposite way is cold, stony silence. Both are meant to intimidate, and both are indicators that anger is on the rise. What should you do when you notice your vocal volume increasing? As trite as it may sound, counting slowly to ten is not a bad idea. It lets your rational mind catch up with your feelings.

Each of these triggers, like the warning lights on your car's dashboard, is an indicator that anger is rising and it's time for you to pause and take inventory of what might be going wrong. The more adept you become at recognizing the triggers, the more effective you'll become at curbing your angry outbursts. Why? Because you will be able to catch your anger before it spirals out of control. These warning signs allow you to remove yourself from the situation for a few minutes or for as long as it takes you to cool down.

Consider a Hassle Log

If you're willing to admit you have a problem with anger, you are sure to find help and improvement by keeping a "hassle log." Therapists often use this technique, but it doesn't take a professional to make it work. The hassle log is a diary-like means of analyzing provocative events. You simply keep a record of all your angry episodes, including places, happenings, persons, what you did or said, the results, how you felt afterward, and what you wish you or the other person had done differently. This simple exercise heightens your awareness of where, when, why, and how often you get angry. This awareness can do more than you might imagine to help you to keep your cool. Keeping a hassle log for just a week could mark a major turning point in your life. It's a simple and proven tool that works wonders for many.

> No man is such a conqueror as the man who has defeated himself.
> **HENRY WARD BEECHER**

Seek Help

If your anger is spiraling out of control despite your putting anger management techniques into practice, or if your anger is getting you into trouble with the law or hurting others—you need more help. There are many therapists, classes, and programs for people with anger management problems. Asking for help is not a sign of weakness. You'll certainly find others in the same shoes, and getting direct feedback on techniques for controlling anger can be tremendously helpful.

Consider professional help if

- **You feel constantly frustrated and angry no matter what management techniques you try.**
- **Your temper causes repeated problems at home or at work.**
- **You have gotten in trouble with the law due to your anger.**
- **Your anger has ever led to physical violence.**

If you don't know why you are getting angry, your anger will continue to be very hard to control. Therapy provides a safe environment in which to learn more about the reasons for your anger and to identify its triggers. It's also a safe place to practice new skills in ways of expressing your anger appropriately.

COPING WITH YOUR ANGRY SPOUSE

You know the phrase. You've seen it on buttons and bumper stickers. "I don't get mad, I get even." For people struggling with chronic anger, this is no joke. They are driven to retaliation and revenge. They want to settle the score. When they feel they have been mistreated, getting back at the offender becomes their driving obsession. They plan countless ways of vindicating themselves, all the while neglecting the ancient wisdom that says "He who seeks revenge, digs two graves."

You can help your angry spouse ease this spiteful outlook. It's often scary when you're on the receiving end of someone's wrath, but just as your spouse needs to learn new ways to cope with impulses toward outbursts, you can benefit from a few strategies yourself. Here are some of the best coping tactics for keeping your cool when your spouse gets hotheaded.

Don't Be a Scapegoat

"Watch out, Mom, kids, cats, and dogs! Here comes Dad, and he's upset again!" is a common attitude in homes where Dad has an anger problem. Why? Because volcanoes erupt most often when and where the angry person feels safest. An angry spouse may actually be upset at his boss or his son or his pastor, for example, but you end up being the brunt of his vengeance because you are a safer target. So if you find yourself continually the object of your spouse's eruptions, it is probably because you are a safe object—a scapegoat.

The term *scapegoat* comes from the Old Testament reference to the innocent goat that was brought to the altar by the high priest.[6] Laying both hands on the goat's head, the high priest confessed all the sins of the people. The goat was then taken into the wilderness and released, thus symbolically taking all the sins of the people into a land that was uninhabited.

Do you ever feel like this goat when you are the object of your spouse's anger? It's not uncommon. Usually you are an innocent bystander, doing nothing wrong, when suddenly you reel under an outburst of anger heaped on your head like red-hot cinders blasted from a violent, volcanic mountain. Understanding this common phenomenon can help you cope with an angry partner in two ways. First, you can take solace in knowing you are not the cause of the anger. Second, you can set boundaries by helping your spouse identify the true object of his wrath. You can say something like, "I know you're expressing your anger at me right now, but I wonder if it's really the situation at work that's making you so emotional." A calm and simple statement like this is sometimes all it takes to put an angry person on his heels and get him to simmer down.

Guard Against Contamination

In his autobiography, *Number 1,* baseball legend Billy Martin told about hunting in Texas with Mickey Mantle. Mickey had a friend who would let them hunt on his ranch. When they reached the ranch, Mickey told Billy to wait in the car while he checked with his friend. Mantle's friend quickly gave them permission to hunt, but he asked Mickey a

> A quick-tempered person does foolish things.
> PROVERBS 14:17

favor. He had a pet mule in the barn, and the animal was going blind. He didn't have the heart to put him out of his misery. He asked Mickey to shoot the mule for him.

When Mickey came back to the car, he pretended to be angry. He scowled and slammed the door. Billy asked him what was wrong, and Mickey said his friend wouldn't let them hunt. "I'm so mad at that guy," Mantle said, "I'm going out to his barn and shoot one of his mules!" Mantle drove like a maniac to the barn. Martin protested, "We can't do that!" But Mickey was adamant. "Just watch me," he shouted.

When they got to the barn, Mantle jumped out of the car with his rifle, ran inside, and shot the mule. As he turned to leave, he heard two shots outside the barn, and he ran back to the car. He saw that Martin had taken out his rifle too. "What are you doing, Martin?" he yelled. Martin yelled back, face red with anger, "We'll show that son of a gun! I just killed two of his cows!"

Anger can be dangerously contagious. As Proverbs puts it, "Do not make friends with a hot-tempered person . . . or you may learn their ways."[7] When you are married to an angry spouse, it's very easy to amp up your own rage just to balance the scales. It's a dangerous strategy and one that only compounds a couple's conflicts. So beware. Guard against anger's contaminating effect.

Don't Go to War Without Understanding the Battle

If you find yourself unwittingly caught in a rancorous tug-of-war with your angry spouse, don't pull out all your artillery before you clearly understand what you are fighting for. Fighting before you understand the battle can cause irreparable damage to relationships and families. Instead, postpone your urge to prove your point and take the time to define clearly what the battle is about. Say to your partner, "I want to be sure I understand what is upsetting you. Is it that . . . ?"

By defining the conflict, you bring some objectivity into it, and that can help you avoid a lot of useless strife. "Never speak in the heat of anger," says Carol Tavris. "You say things badly or wrongly. Give yourself time to cool off, because you want your anger to accomplish something."

SAY GOOD-BYE TO CRAZY

Mel Gibson is not the only one to have his angry outbursts made public. In February 2009, a twenty-seven-year-old woman from Fort Pierce, Florida, walked into a McDonald's restaurant and ordered a ten-piece McNuggets meal.[8] You know how it is when you're hungry and you have a craving for something particular. Your imagination starts working and you can almost taste those McNuggets before you order them.

Well, that's when things got really tough for this hungry woman. The McDonald's employee behind the counter took the order and received payment only to discover that they were out of those bite-sized, warm, tasty McNuggets. The employee told the customer that she would have to order something else from the menu. The customer asked for her money back. The employee said all sales are final, but she could have a higher-priced item from the menu if she wanted.

No, the McNuggets-loving woman insisted, she wanted Mc-Nuggets—not a Big Mac, not a McRib, not a Quarter Pounder. She was angry, this was clearly an emergency, and she knew what to do in an emergency: she took out her cell phone and called 911 to complain. Apparently the 911 workers didn't take her seriously, because she called them three times to get help!

The woman never received any McNuggets, but she did get a ticket from the police for misusing 911.

Does this story sound bizarre? Incidents just as crazy occur all the time. When we get angry, major perspective distortions skew our sense of judgment, and we act in crazy ways. Road rage caused by something as simple as failing to dim one's headlights can result in a shooting. Anger twists our perspective. It skews our judgment. Anger makes

> Keep cool; anger is not an argument.
> DANIEL WEBSTER

small things big and big things small. When we're angry, having to eat a burger instead of McNuggets swells into a disaster of major proportions, while calling 911 and tying up a vital line meant for life-or-death emergencies shrinks to a matter of insignificance.

Whether you are trying to manage your anger or living with a person who is, know that uncontrolled anger is a serious problem with serious consequences. The good news is that you can avoid those consequences. You don't have to let anger make you crazy like Miss McNugget, like Mel Gibson, or like a driver who pulls a gun on a person who won't let him change lanes. Anger can ruin one's life, and it certainly ruins marriages. But it doesn't have to happen. Anger can be managed and controlled. It can become an asset instead of a destructive liability that makes you do crazy things. Getting the proper help and finding a solution is essential to the sanity of your relationship.

We don't pretend to think that this appendix can suddenly solve all your anger issues. We're simply giving you a starting place to help you begin the process of saying good-bye to the craziness of out-of-control anger in your home.

★ NOTES ★

Introduction: When the Fur Flies

1. See http://www.mydaily.com/2011/03/11/fighting-fair-how-to-fight-fair/.

2. Jerry Stiller, *Married to Laughter: A Love Story Featuring Anne Meara* (New York: Simon & Schuster, 2000).

Chapter 1: What Most Couples Don't Know About Conflict

1. D. J. Canary, W. R. Cupach, and R. T. Serpe, "A Competence-Based Approach to Examining Interpersonal Conflict," *Communication Research* 28 (2001): 79–104.

2. "Fair feud? 6 issues couples should argue about: 'Men's Health' on which arguments can ruin or strengthen relationships," NBC News, August 20, 2007, http://today.msnbc.msn.com/id/20323044.

3. Unhealthy conflict makes married couples more susceptible to illness and even prolongs the healing process of a wound.

4. K. T. Buehlman and John Gottman, "The Oral History Coding System," in *What Predicts Divorce?: The Measures*, ed. John Gottman (Hillsdale, NJ: Erlbaum, 1996).

5. Proverbs 13:10, NLT.

6. M. Argyle and A. Furnham, "Sources of Satisfaction and Conflict in Long-Term Relationships," *Journal of Marriage and the Family* 45 (1983): 481–493.

7. Paula Szuchman and Jenny Anderson, *Spousonomics: Using Economics to Master Love, Marriage and Dirty Dishes* (New York: Random House, 2011).

8. Rachel A. Simmons, Peter C. Gordon, and Dianne L. Chambless, "Pronouns in Marital Interaction: What Do 'You' and 'I'

Say About Marital Health?" *Psychological Science* 16, no. 12 (2005): 932–936.

Chapter 2: The Surprising Benefits of a Good Fight

1. H. Markman, S. Stanley, and S. L. Blumberg, "Fighting for Your Marriage: Positive Steps for Preventing Divorce and Preserving a Lasting Love" (New York: Jossey-Bass, 1994).

2. *Shrek 2*, directed by Andrew Adamson, Kelly Asbury, and Conrad Vernon (Universal City: Dreamworks SKG, 2004).

3. B. R. Karney and T. N. Bradbury, "The Longitudinal Course of Marital Quality and Stability: A Review of Theory, Methods, and Research," *Psychological Bulletin* 118 (1995): 3–34.

Chapter 3: What You're *Really* Fighting About

1. "The Can Opener," *Everybody Loves Raymond*, September 27, 1999, written by Philip Rosenthal, Aaron Shure, and Susan Van Allen, directed by Will Mackenzie (Burbank: CBS, 1999).

2. Skit written by Clark Cothern, Ypsilanti, Michigan, July 3, 2005.

3. Keith Sanford et al., "Perceived Threat and Perceived Neglect: Couples' Underlying Concerns During Conflict," *Psychological Assessment* 22, no. 2 (2010): 288.

Chapter 4: What Is Your Conflict Quotient?

1. A. L. Vangelisti and S. L. Young, "When Words Hurt: The Effects of Perceived Intentionality on Interpersonal Relationships," *Journal of Social and Personal Relationships* 17 (2000): 393–424.

2. J. K. Kiecolt-Glaser, W. B. Malarkey, M. A. Chee, T. Newton, J. T. Cacioppo, H. Y. Mao, and R. Glaser, "Negative Behavior During Marital Conflict Is Associated with Immunological Down-Regulation," *Psychosomatic Medicine* 55 (1993): 395–409.

3. John Milton, *Paradise Lost*, 1.254–255.

4. Some people, of course, never learn to manage their anger. This leads to unspeakable pain and anguish in marriage. When a person's angry emotions run amok in a relationship, conflicts get scary. If unmanaged anger is a factor in your marriage conflicts, the appen-

dix is dedicated to helping you overcome that problem.

5. Romans 12:2.

Chapter 5: The Rules of Fight Club

1. K. L. Johnson and M. E. Roloff, "Correlates of the Perceived Resolvability and Relational Consequences of Serial Arguing in Dating Relationships: Argumentative Features and the Use of Coping Strategies," *Journal of Social and Personal Relationships* 17 (2000): 676–686.

2. http://couplestraininginstitute.com/gottman-couples-and-marital-therapy/.

3. Beverly Engel, *The Power of Apology* (New York: John Wiley & Sons, 2001).

4. John M. Gottman and Clifford I. Notarius, "Decade Review: Observing Marital Interaction," *Journal of Marriage and the Family* 62 (November 2000): 927–947.

5. Lisa S. Matthews, K. A. S. Wickrama, and Rand D. Conger, "Predicting Marital Instability from Spouse and Observer Reports of Marital Interaction," *Journal of Marriage and Family* 58, no. 3 (August 1996): 641–655.

6. Robert W. Levenson and John M. Gottman, "Physiological and Affective Predictors of Change in Relationship Satisfaction," *Journal of Personality and Social Psychology* 49, no. 1 (July 1985): 85–94.

7. J. L. Smith, W. Ickes, J. Hall, and S. D. Hodges, eds., *Managing Interpersonal Sensitivity: Knowing When—and When Not—to Understand Others* (New York: Nova Science, 2011).

8. N. M. Lambert, S. M. Graham, and F. D. Fincham, "Understanding the Layperson's Perception of Prayer: A Prototype Analysis of Prayer," *Psychology of Religion and Spirituality* 3 (2011): 55–65.

9. Christopher G. Ellison, "Family Ties, Friendships, and Subjective Well-Being Among Black Americans," *Journal of Marriage and the Family* 52 (1990): 298–310.

10. Neal Krause, "Praying for Others, Financial Strain, and

Physical Health Status in Late Life," *Journal for the Scientific Study of Religion* 42 (2003): 377–391.

Chapter 6: Uncovering Your Personal Fight Type

1. Ben Dattner, "Credit and Blame at Work," *Psychology Today*, June 13, 2008, http://www.psychologytoday.com/blog/minds-work/200806/the-use-and-misuse-personality-tests-coaching-and-development.

2. Timothy Keller and Kathy Keller, *The Meaning of Marriage: Facing the Complexities of Commitment with the Wisdom of God* (New York: Dutton, 2011), 145–146.

3. "Man Uses Air Raid Siren to Quiet Wife," CNN.com, April 19, 2003.

Chapter 7: Leveraging Your Fight Types Together

1. William Shakespeare, *Hamlet*, 1.3.78–82.

2. Henry David Thoreau, *Walden*

Chapter 8: Fighting Through the Big Five

1. Greg Evans, "Seinfeld's *Marriage Ref*: Nada Nada Nada," *The Huffington Post*, March 1, 2010, http://www.huffingtonpost.com/greg-evans/seinfelds-emmarriage-refe_b_480471.html.

2. *Market Watch*, "AICPA Survey: Finances Causing Rifts for American Couples," *Wall Street Journal*, May 19, 2012.

3. Financial Behavior and Attitudes, Money Habitudes, http://www.moneyhabitudes.com/about/press-news/financial-behavior-and-attitudes-statistics/.

4. Catherine Rampell, "Money Fights Predict Divorce Rates," *New York Times*, December 7, 2009, http://economix.blogs.nytimes.com/2009/12/07/money-fights-predict-divorce-rates/.

5. Vanessa Ko, "French Man Forced to Pay Ex-Wife a Settlement for Lack of Sex," *Time*, September 6, 2011, http://newsfeed.time.com/2011/09/06/french-man-forced-to-pay-ex-wife-a-settlement-for-lack-of-sex/#ixzz21tTF4UcH.

6. http://www.time.com/time/subscriber/article/0,33009,981624-2,00.html.

7. Kaplan, R. H (1987). "Lottery winners: The myth and reality." *Journal of Gambling Behavior*, 3, pp 168-178.

8. Michelle Healy and Alejandro Gonzalez, *"Setting a Date for Date Night,"* USA Today, May 2, 2009; based on the Frigidaire Motherload Index.

9. A. Aron, C. C. Norman, E. N. Aron, C. McKenna, and R. Heyman, "Couples Shared Participation in Novel and Arousing Activities and Experienced Relationship Quality," *Journal of Personality and Social Psychology* 78 (2000): 273–283.

10. "Becoming Parents: It's More than Having a Baby," University of Washington School of Nursing, http://nursing.uw.edu/newsroom/press-releases/becoming-parents-its-more-than-having-a-baby.html.

11. Frank Pompa, "Why People Have Kids?" *USA Today*, May 6, 2010.

12. Sari Harrar and Rita DeMaria, "Let Parenthood Strengthen Your Marriage," *Reader's Digest*, http://www.rd.com/advice/parenting/let-parenthood-strengthen-your-marriage.

13. Belinda Luscombe, "What a Chore: Housework Is Bad for Both Sexes," *Time*, May 23, 2011, http://healthland.time.com/2011/05/23/housework-bad-for-both-sexes.

14. Jeanna Bryner, "Key to Successful Marriage: Say 'Thank You,'" *Live Science*, July 27, 2007, http://www.livescience.com/4556-key-successful-marriage.html.

Chapter 9: The Fight That Can Save Your Marriage

1. *Just Married*, written by Sam Harper, directed by Shawn Levy (Los Angeles: Twentieth Century Fox Film Corporation, 2003).

2. http://www.oprah.com/relationships/uncovering-childhood-wounds.

3. Harville Hendrix and Helen LaKelly Hunt, "The Marriage Repair Kit," Oprah.com, http://www.oprah.com/relationships/Uncovering-Childhood-Wounds

4. *As Good as It Gets*, written by Mark Andrus and James L. Brooks, directed by James L. Brooks (Culver City: Tristar Pictures,

1997).

Conclusion: Keeping the Peace

1. Joshua Wolf Shenk, "What Makes Us Happy?" *The Atlantic* (June 2009): 36–53.

Appendix: Controlling Anger Before It Controls You

1. Tavris, C. (1982). *Anger: The Misunderstood Emotion.* Simon and Schuster, New York.

2. Proverbs 29:11.

3. L. R. Huesmann, L. R. "Stability of Aggression over Time and Generations," *Developmental Psychology,* 20, (1984): 1120–1134.

4. Associated Press, "Man hits woman on way to anger control class," March 1, 2008, NBCNews.com, http://www.msnbc.msn.com/id/23421960/ns/us_news-weird_news/t/man-hits-woman-way-anger-control-class/#.UMk4nI5DGxowww.msnbc.com.

5. Associated Press, "Ten Percent of U.S. Drivers Have Their 'Check Engine' Light On," www.yahoonews.com, June 10, 2008; "Snapshots: How long the light's been on," *USA Today,* June 22, 2008.

6. Leviticus 16:20–22.

7. Proverbs 22:24–25.

8. Associated Press, "Florida woman calls 911 3 times over McNuggets," www.news.yahoo.com, March 4, 2009.

★ ABOUT THE AUTHORS ★

Drs. Les and Leslie Parrott are #1 *New York Times* best-selling authors and the founders of the Center for Relationship Development at Seattle Pacific University (SPU). Les is a psychologist and Leslie is a marriage and family therapist at SPU. The Parrotts are authors of *Real Relationships, Crazy Good Sex, L.O.V.E., Your Time-Starved Marriage, Love Talk,* and the Gold Medallion Award–winning *Saving Your Marriage Before It Starts.* The Parrotts have been featured on *Oprah, CBS This Morning,* CNN, and *The View* and in *USA Today* and the *New York Times.* They are also frequent guest speakers and have written for a variety of magazines. The Parrott's website, LesandLeslie.com, features more than one thousand free video-on-demand pieces answering relationship questions. Les and Leslie live in Seattle, Washington, with their two young sons.

THIS CHANGES EVERYTHING
THE GOOD FIGHT APP

It's powerful, fun and FREE (reg. $12)
with the purchase of the book.

Your smartphone (iPhone or Android) will soon be essential to helping you
fight a good fight. In it you'll find videos, assessments, games and more that
will help you personalize the content of this book.

To get the app on your smartphone, visit **www.GoodFight.us**

THE GOOD FIGHT
VIDEO KIT
FOR COUPLES CLASSES

This engaging and fun DVD (with workbooks) is ideal for couples' classes
and groups. You'll laugh while you learn how conflict can bring you closer.

Learn more at LesandLeslie.com

SAVING YOUR MARRIAGE BEFORE IT STARTS

This is more than a book—it's practically a self-guided premarital counseling course, and it is used by counselors and churches everywhere. Make your marriage everything it is meant to be....over a million couples already have!

"It was easy, fun and taught us so much!"
-Rachel M, Indiana

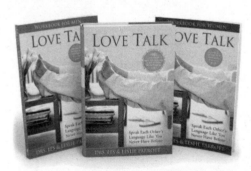

LOVE TALK

Love Talk is a deep yet simple plan full of new insights to revolutionize relationships. Crack the code on your unique "talk styles" and speak each other's language like never before.

"Amazing! Almost immediately we began to notice a difference in our conversations." -Kevin, San Diego

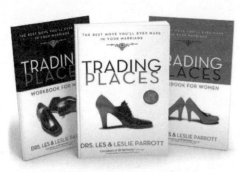

TRADING PLACES

Trading Places reduces conflict, deepens your commitment, and helps you live as better friends and lovers. Mutual empathy—the revolutionary tool for instantly improving a relationship—can be learned and practiced.

"Excellent. Empathy is a must and this book oozes with how to get it and keep it in your marriage." -Emmie, Nashville

REAL RELATIONSHIPS

Learn how to make your bad relationships better and your good relationships great. Bridge the gender gap. Forge friendships that last. Instantly improve your "Love IQ." Relate to God without feeling phony. Your relationships will never be the same.

"This is the best relatoinship guide I have ever found!"
-Cindy, Dallas

WORTHY®
PUBLISHING

If you enjoyed this book will you consider sharing the message with others?

- Mention the book in a Facebook post, Twitter update, Pinterest pin, or blog post.

- Recommend this book to those in your small group, book club, workplace, and classes.

- Head over to facebook.com/lesandleslieparrott, "LIKE" the page, and post a comment as to what you enjoyed the most.

- Tweet "I recommend reading #TheGoodFight by @LesParrott // @worthypub"

- Pick up a copy for someone you know who would be challenged and encouraged by this message.

- Write a review on amazon.com, bn.com, goodreads.com, or cbd.com.

You can subscribe to Worthy Publishing's newsletter at worthypublishing.com.

WORTHY PUBLISHING
FACEBOOK PAGE

WORTHY PUBLISHING
WEBSITE